THE FEDERAL INTEREST IN HIGHER EDUCATION

Education is here placed among the articles of public care, not that it would be proposed to take its ordinary branches out of the hands of private enterprise, which manages so much better all the concerns to which it is equal; but a public institution can alone supply those sciences which, though rarely called for, are yet necessary to complete the circle, all the parts of which contribute to the improvement of the country, and some of them to its preservation.

Thomas Jefferson to the Congress of the United States, 2 December, 1806

THE FEDERAL INTEREST
IN HIGHER EDUCATION

HOMER D. BABBIDGE, Jr.,
and
ROBERT M. ROSENZWEIG

McGRAW-HILL BOOK COMPANY, INC.   1962

New York   San Francisco   Toronto   London

THE FEDERAL INTEREST IN HIGHER EDUCATION

To Marcia Babbidge and Adelle Rosenzweig

PREFACE

This volume deals with a complex set of relationships between the Federal Government, on the one hand, and American higher education, on the other. It is a subject about which there are inevitable differences of opinion, and one that can be viewed from every point on the educational and political compass.

It may be (as one of the readers of this book in manuscript has suggested) that the authors view their subject too much as insiders, from a vantage point too close to the "true north" of bureaucracy. And certainly it should be understood that, while we have both had some experience at the institutional end of the relationship we seek to explore, we have for the past several years been in the Federal Government.

No doubt this fact of personal biography colors our views in some respects. We trust it will be clear to the reader, however, that we have written neither an apologia for Government policies and practices nor an assault upon those of educational institutions. The facts of the relationship between the two do not warrant either.

Indeed we have not undertaken to attack or defend anyone. Rather, our goal in writing this book has been to provoke—to provoke concern and discussion among those who are parties to the relationship and among those who are deeply affected by it but least aware of it—the public at large. We hope that what we have written will have this effect because we believe that higher education is important; that the people of the United States have a vital stake in its strength and vitality; that this stake has become increasingly manifest in the actions of the Federal Government; and that this important area of public policy—like all others in our system of government—must be fully and freely debated by an informed citizenry.

We stress particularly the last—the crucial importance of an enlightened public. Therefore, we have tried to sketch the background and development of relations between the Government and the higher-education community and to describe the present status of those relations and the readiness and capacity of each party to deal with the other. We have tried, too, to evaluate three of the major issues—obstacles if you will—in the maturing of the relationship; and we have tried, finally, to look to the future. In all this our object has been to see and to write as realistically as we can.

Above all—and perhaps this is really the "point" of our effort— we hope we have conveyed a sense of the process of government in a free society; of its delicate balances, its stubborn insistence on shades of gray, rather than either black or white, and its marvelous potential, if properly used, for constructive effort.

In some respects this book represents an early exploration of a subject as uncharted as it is vast. The authors have been grateful, therefore, for the comments and advice of a number of highly knowledgeable pioneers both in and out of the Government. Without intending to make them responsible in any way for the views expressed by the authors, we are anxious nonetheless to record our gratitude to the Messrs. Reginald G. Conley, Associate General Counsel of the U.S. Department of Health, Education, and Welfare; Charles G. Dobbins, Staff Associate of the American Council on Education; Ralph C. M. Flynt, Assistant U.S. Commissioner of Education; John W. Gardner, President of the Carnegie Corporation of New York; David D. Henry, President of the University of Illinois; Charles V. Kidd, Associate Director of the National Institues of Health; J. Kenneth Little, former Deputy U.S. Commissioner of Education and Vice President of the University of Wisconsin; and Russell D. Thackrey, Executive Secretary of The American Association of Land-Grant Colleges and State Universities. We are most appreciative also of the valuable assistance rendered in the preparation of the manuscript by Miss Doris McMahon, Mrs. Elfrida L. Warf, and Mr. James B. Jones, Jr. The enormous debt we owe our wives is, we trust, acknowledged, if not paid, in the dedication of this volume.

Homer D. Babbidge, Jr.
Robert M. Rosenzweig

CONTENTS

ix

CHAPTER ONE

HISTORIC FEDERAL INTEREST IN HIGHER EDUCATION

For all the air of recency that permeates discussions of the role of the Federal Government in higher education, the subject has a rather considerable historical background. With no pretense of thoroughness, the following notes are offered to suggest some of the evolutionary background of a modern issue and a subject of considerable current interest: the relationship of the Federal Government to American higher education.

Education and the Constitution

Much importance has been attached to the fact that the Constitution of the United States makes no reference to education. Indeed, the word education does not appear in that document. Since authority to legislate regarding education is not listed among the enumerated powers specifically granted to the Government of the United States, and in the light of the Tenth Amendment to the Constitution, the view has been widely held that responsibility for education is exclusively reserved to the States. Since the Congress has enacted scores of laws affecting education, and in view of the fact that a significant proportion of the educational and general income of colleges and universities in the United States is now derived from the Federal Government, it may be highly aca-

1

demic but nonetheless interesting to inquire briefly into some of the reasons for the Constitution's silence on the subject of education.

There is certainly no reason to assume any lack of interest in the subject of education on the part of the authors of the Constitution of 1787. The principal authors, in fact, were almost without exception keenly and actively interested in the subject. A number of them had identified education as a legitimate object of concern to the Federal Government. James Madison, for example, listed the inability of the Congress to legislate upon matters of education as one of those several weaknesses of the Articles of Confederation that warranted the calling of the Constitutional Convention and the creation of a stronger central government. The constitutional historian Max Farrand identifies constitutional silence on the subject of education as one of the "few exceptions" to his thesis that "every known defect of the Confederation" was dealt with in the writing of the new Constitution.

The provision of the Northwest Ordinance of 1785 reserving one square mile of each township for the maintenance of public schools is frequently cited as another evidence of an early national and even Federal interest in education. Economic historians have tended to take the view that this provision was designed more to encourage development of the Western lands (by making them seem more attractive to Eastern investors) than as an evidence of concern for education as such. It is nonetheless true that the National Government in this early stage of its development assumed the authority, even under the "weak" Articles of Confederation, to legislate upon the subject of education.

The question of whether or not the Federal Government had authority to legislate with regard to education within the several States as such (as opposed to territories not a part of any State) did not arise until later. It appears evident, given the wording of the Constitution and given the Tenth Amendment thereto, that responsibility for education within the States was intended to rest with the States. The question remains, however, whether or not, in failing to enumerate education as among the areas of concern of the Federal Government, the Constitutional Convention consciously regarded the alternative as being exclusive State responsibility for and authority over matters of education.

There seems to be at least one instance in the Convention debate itself that suggests that a majority of those present did not regard education as being among the legitimate concerns of the Federal Government. Late in the debate over the document it was proposed that authority to create a National University should be included among the enumerated powers. The decision not to include this item seems to have rested upon the assumption that such a university would be established within the Federal District, over which the Constitution already had declared the Federal Government sovereign. It is in a sense ironic that this one concrete evidence that the Convention did not regard education as a matter of Federal responsibility should at the same time be an evidence of that body's great interest in higher education.

It remains a question, however, whether the Constitutional Convention was conscious of the alternative that has emerged in subsequent history. The plain fact of the matter is that, at the time of the creation of the new Constitution, there was no such thing as State responsibility for education. In higher education, responsibility was almost exclusively in the hands of religious bodies and private citizens. In the fields of elementary and secondary education, such public responsibility as there was had been assumed by towns and local communities, not by States. It would be many decades after the creation of the new Constitution before anything resembling State assumption of responsibility for education would emerge. The nonpublic flavor of education at the time has prompted one historian to observe that a proposal for Federal *or* State responsibility for education would have elicited a question as to which *church* should control it.[1]

The possibility that education was not regarded either as a

proper matter of Federal concern or of State concern is given credence in a number of instances, but perhaps most interestingly in President Jefferson's message to the Congress of 1806. In a discussion of the somewhat quaint problem of disposing of Federal surplus monies, Jefferson was moved to suggest that some of the surplus funds be expended for education. He proposed that authority to expend Federal funds for the "great purposes" of public education, roads, rivers, and canals be added to the constitutional enumeration of Federal powers. Jefferson acknowledged that an amendment to the Constitution would probably be necessary, not because the States were exercising responsibility for public education, but simply because, in a constitutional sense, education was not among the objects then enumerated. Jefferson's statement is worthy of careful reading:

> Education is here placed among the articles of public care, not that it would be proposed to take its ordinary branches out of the hands of private enterprise, which manages so much better all the concerns to which it is equal; but a public institution can alone supply those sciences which, though rarely called for, are yet necessary to complete the circle, all the parts of which contribute to the improvement of the country, and some of them to its preservation.

It is Jefferson's reference to "private enterprise" that is of interest here. Clearly, his suggestion that the Federal Government assume some responsibility for public education was not cast in the context of usurping power from the States. Conceding education in "its ordinary branches" to the religious and private bodies which at that time and to all intent and purposes had exclusive responsibility for education in the United States, he proposed a complementary role for the Federal Government.

A National University

The observations of Jefferson and other early leaders of the Republic suggest a clear distinction in their minds between the "ordinary branches" of education and higher education. Virtually all discussion of the Federal role in education centered, in the early years of the Republic, upon the possible establishment of a National University. In their great concern for the development of national leadership, many of the Founding Fathers had urged a departure from the frequently narrow and parochial views of local custom, habit, and education.

It was important in the view of Washington, Noah Webster, and Jefferson, among others, to provide American youth with a satisfactory alternative to European education.[2] The alternative, in order to be acceptable, must be more than the limited, parochial effort of one of the Colonies or States. For one thing, given the limited intellectual resources of the new Nation, only a National University could provide sufficiently sophisticated instruction in the "higher branches" of learning. For another, the advocates of a National University clearly felt that it would lend prestige to the young Nation and serve as a symbolic evidence of the American aspiration to be great "in arts as in arms."

Persistently during the first quarter century of the newly reorganized Government, the several Presidents urged upon the Congress the creation of a National University. George Washington even willed 50 shares of stock in the Potomac Canal Company for the purpose, though the whereabouts of this bequest remain a mystery to this day. Interest in the proposal has risen and fallen during the subsequent years. The acceptance in 1867 of Mr. James Smithson's bequest "to found . . . an establishment for the increase and diffusion of knowledge among men" came closest to the establishment of a National University, but a National University as such has never materialized. For our purposes here it is important only to note the early and persistent notion that a Federal institution was necessary to "complete the circle" of higher learning in the United States.[3]

Early Schemes for American Education

The idea of a National University was a frequent and sometimes central feature of a number of early grand schemes for the development of a system of education for the United States. Jefferson had been a leader in identifying the critical interdependence of education and democracy, and his friend du Pont de Nemours was one of the early planners of a system to implement the notion. Benjamin Rush, Noah Webster, James Sullivan, Robert Coran, Nathaniel Chipman, and others joined in the popular pastime of laying out a plan of education for the new Republic. Indeed, the American Philosophical Society conducted a contest in 1796, offering a prize for the best plan of education for the new Nation, and elicited a number of proposals of varying quality and ingenuity.

Such writings of the period were understandably cast in the grandiosity of a new Republic and varied greatly in their degree of specificity. They had in common, however, two characteristics that give them significance in the context of this discussion. First, they all proceeded from the assumption that broad education was essential to the successful operation of the new Nation. Further, the authors argued that the government of free people had a stake in, and a degree of responsibility for, the provision of such education. If they were uncertain as to where within government the locus of responsibility was to be placed, it was more out of ignorance of any history of government activity than because they had preconceived notions of local or State control. The idea of any government actually taking over responsibility for education was new enough; to designate the agency of government might have seemed to them presumptuous. All agreed, however, beyond question, that what should be done in education should be done throughout all States.

The Concept of National Needs

Among those "sciences which, though rarely called for, are yet necessary . . . to the improvement of the country, and some of them to its preservation" to which Jefferson referred was, of course, the science of war. The establishment in 1802 of the United States Military Academy at West Point, New York, was an early indication that the Federal Government, in seeking highly skilled manpower with which to carry out the legitimate objects of concern of the Federal Government, would be willing to engage in and support educational activities toward this end. And though West Point was not authorized by Congress to award a collegiate-level degree until 1933, it offered instruction of a type and kind not only important to the national defense, but unavailable at existing institutions of higher education. President Francis Wayland of Brown University was probably correct when he observed in 1850 that every engineered bridge and highway in the United States had been constructed under the direction of graduates of that single institution, West Point. Some sixty years after the establishment of the U.S. Military Academy, and amidst concern for military needs during the Civil War, the Congress would add to the functions of the land-grant institutions the provision of instruction in military tactics. The subsequent proliferation of "reserve-officer training" and of service academies themselves was but an extension of the principle established early in the Union, namely, that the expenditure of Federal funds for educational purposes and the use of educational institutions were justified in the effort to produce highly or uniquely trained personnel to meet identifiable needs of the National Government. Much of the subsequent history of Federal involvement in American higher education constitutes nothing more than a broadening of the definitions embodied in this concept.

Public vs. Private Institutions

Between the founding of West Point in 1802 and the enactment of the so-called land-grant legislation in 1862, Federal legislative activities in the field of education were limited to those provisions embodied in laws enabling the admission of new States. But during these six decades, an impressive amount of educational activity was under way throughout the Nation. In elementary and secondary education, strong movements were afoot, especially in Massachusetts, Connecticut, and Rhode Island, to provide free schooling at public expense. In the field of higher education, the westward movement of population invited a variety of churches to follow in its wake, and it was virtually axiomatic that each new community founded under religious auspices should have its own college. President Wayland of Brown University observed that control and direction of higher education by sectarian interests were "taken for granted." "Let a religious body resolve to establish a college anywhere," President Lindsley of Nashville declared in 1829, "and, in a few months, you shall hear that they have some fifty or a hundred thousand dollars to commence with." Out of the 172 surviving colleges founded in the United States prior to the Civil War, 150 were under private auspices. Only three of the institutions of higher learning in the United States founded prior to 1800 were public.

There was, however, growing sentiment in favor of public control of institutions of higher education. The famous Dartmouth College Case of 1819 not only represented the first instance in which the Supreme Court of the United States acted on an educational question, but the decision in this Case also profoundly affected the course of subsequent patterns of support in higher education. It will be recalled that the Case came to the attention of the Court as a result of efforts on the part of the Legislature of the State of New Hampshire to gain control of what was in effect a private institution. The Court's decision upholding the sanctity of the College's Royal Charter constituted a foundation stone of the legal concept of the inviolability of charters and contracts, and it also made demonstrably clear to all concerned that public institutions of higher education could not be created by the simple act of taking control of private institutions. As a consequence of this decision, the Nation saw no further significant public efforts to take over private institutions or to impose the public will upon private institutions.[4] The decision in fact encouraged private patrons in their efforts to establish institutions independent of government, and at the same time it stimulated a pronounced effort to bring into being institutions created by the people and for the people. To this single decision of the Supreme Court of the United States can largely be traced our present patterns of institutional support and control.

The Land-Grant Acts

It was the failure of the existing institutions, largely under private or religious control, but even including State universities,[5] to respond to popular will and wishes that led to the most noted and significant Federal action in the field of higher education during the nineteenth century. The so-called land-grant colleges were brought into being to provide a form of higher education not sympathetically viewed by established institutions and not available under circumstances that made it accessible to large numbers of people. The period from 1800 to 1860 in higher education in the United States has properly been called a period of "intellectual crosscurrents." A good many new ideas were being developed, and considerable public ferment was evident, but no action on a significant scale was taken during this period to redirect the course of American higher education. The action of the Federal Government in creating the land-grant institutions had the effect, when viewed in one light, of converting an eddying pool of crosscurrents into at least one stream that had direction and force. This bold action is of more than academic interest since it required that the Congress act on a dramatic scale in an area which, in the hindsight of constitutional doctrine, might have been presumed to fall outside the scope of authority of the Federal Government.

The claims of the supporters of Jonathan Baldwin Turner notwithstanding, Representative (later Senator) Justin Morrill of Vermont is considered the Father of the Land-Grant College Act. Morrill's original intention had been to follow the concept of the National University and the model of West Point in establishing "one or more national agricultural schools upon the basis of the U.S. Naval and Military Schools, in order that one scholar from each Congressional district and two from each State-at-large, may receive a scientific and practical education at public expense." Frustrated in this effort, Morrill later turned to a public land-grant concept, and succeeded in getting enacted into law, with President Lincoln's signature, in 1862, an act which granted public lands for specific educational purposes; a significant grant of land, income from the sale or use of which was to constitute an endowment of a college of Agriculture and the Mechanic Arts. The grant was made not just to new States (as in the case of earlier Congressional actions) and not just in the cases of States which had Federal public lands within their boundaries, but to all States in the Union.

Much of the rationale for the Morrill Land-Grant Act of 1862 was based upon an acknowledged need for instruction in the agricultural and mechanic arts (the latter an emerging concept of the practical application of engineering and the sciences) in a Nation whose agricultural enterprise was growing to enormous proportions and whose economy was beginning to feel the effects of the great Industrial Revolution. It is important to note, however, that the legislation as enacted, while giving particular emphasis to study in these fields (and in military tactics), placed no restrictions or limitations upon the institutions to be created for these purposes. The enabling legislation specifically authorized instruction in other fields deemed to be of value to the industrial and working classes (which was subsequently interpreted to mean any and all fields of study). The authorizing legislation did not even require that the beneficiary institutions, or the institutions created as a result of this legislation, be public in support or control. The Massachusetts Institute of Technology in Massachusetts and Cornell University in New York State, both generally regarded as private institutions, continue to this day to receive funds under the Land-Grant Act and subsequent related legislation. In addition, a number of other institutions, such as Yale University and Brown University, were originally designated as land-grant beneficiaries, but subsequently discontinued their participation in the program.[6]

Out of the land-grant legislation of 1862 emerged two principles that have loomed large in the subsequent history of relations between the Federal Government and higher education. On the one hand, the rationale of the legislation was based upon national needs for trained manpower, in certain specified fields of study, though it recognized the importance of academic autonomy on the part of beneficiary institutions. Secondly, in not limiting benefits of the land-grant legislation to public institutions, it served as a precedent for all subsequent Federal legislation. With only one doubtful exception, the Public Works Administration Program of the Depression period, no Federal program authorized by the Congress has ever made any distinction between public and private institutions of higher education. Such grants, contracts, or other benefits as have been made available to institutions of higher education have been made available on an identical basis to both public and private institutions.

So notable was the success of the Agricultural and Mechanic Arts colleges created by the Congress in 1862, that the Congress took steps before the close of the century to strengthen them greatly. Through the development of an extensive agricultural research program, and through the reorganization of the agricultural extension services on their campuses, the Federal Government gave these institutions a primacy in the field of agriculture which they maintain to this day. Additionally, in 1890, the Congress enacted permanent legislation, under the terms of which annual sums are appropriated to the institutions for instructional purposes. In subsequent provisions through 1960, the amounts thus made available annually approximate $14 million a year. A unique relationship has been developed between the Federal Government and this group of (now) 67 institutions. On the eve of their centennial, they constitute an evidence of what Federal-institutional relationships can be. There has never been a serious charge of Federal interference or Federal control over these institutions. Indeed, there has never even been an employee of the Federal Government whose full time has been required to administer this legislation.

A Federal Agency

The action of the Congress in 1867, in establishing a United States Bureau of Education, must be viewed in the context of a flurry of legislative proposals, only some of which resulted in legislative action, during the period surrounding the Civil War. According to popular legend, Henry Barnard, then Secretary of the Board of Education in Rhode Island, came to Washington in search of information regarding the status of schools in the United States. He was reportedly astonished to learn that there was nowhere in the Nation's capital any repository of such information or any persons knowledgeable in such matters. Largely as a result of Barnard's individual lobbying efforts, and in part because of a growing concern about the simple problem of keeping track of what was going on in a rapidly growing Nation, the Office of Education was brought into being. It was established primarily as an agency for the gathering and dissemination of factual information about the state of education in the United States. The basic authorizing legislation would, however, suggest that its creators anticipated that its duties might develop beyond the scope of simple information gathering and dissemination. Language authorizing the Office to "otherwise promote the cause of education" seemed to give the fledgling agency a wide area for operation. Henry Barnard's willingness to accept the appointment as the first United States Commissioner of Education further suggets that the assignment was not considered an insignificant one.

The historical development of the Office of Education is itself a kind of barometer of Federal interest in and concern for higher education. Established originally as a Department headed by a Secretary, it was soon (1869) relegated to Office, and later Bureau, status in the Department of the Interior. At various times it has been in an independent agency (1939–1953) and at others a stepchild of Departments. Its recent development has been attributed to its status within a Department that gives it central acknowledgment, and this in turn to a rising Federal interest in education.

The National Education Association has long contended that the Office should enjoy cabinet status and has been supported in this view by the reports of a variety of commissions and individuals. It is exceedingly interesting to note, however, that no comparable organization in higher education has ever recommended the elevation of the Office to Departmental status. Whatever the merits of the case, the existence of a Federal Office of Education of almost a century's standing is a concrete evidence of Federal interest; its uncertain locus within the Federal structure evidences at least a degree of uncertainty about the extent and nature of that Federal interest.

Wartime Emergencies

Despite the existence of the Military and Naval Academies (and following the establishment of the Army Medical School in 1893 and the Army War College in 1901), the Federal Government turned to the colleges and universities of the Nation on the eve of World War I in an effort to train additional military officers. Experience with the National Defense Act of 1916, which founded the Reserve Officers' Training Corps, was sufficiently satisfactory so that the Government again turned to and utilized this device during the even greater emergency of World War II. In neither circumstance did anyone question the right of the Armed Forces to take responsibility for the training of their officers, and no question was raised that the Services elected to do this through established institutions rather than in additional Federal institutions created for the purpose. Indeed, with universal military conscription at the time of World War II, the Nation's colleges and universities were faced with the very serious threat of having to close down for want of students, and the availability of Federal funds and federally deployed students for military-training purposes was most welcome. Even peaceably minded institutions like Swarthmore College, though not without debate and some dissatisfaction, elected to turn over to the Military large segments of their campuses and facilities for the purpose of training military officers. A workable compromise between the specific training needs of the military services and the traditional values and practices of the institutions themselves was developed for these purposes. Virtually every four-year college campus in the United States became almost overnight an encampment of uniformed military personnel. It is no exaggeration to say that without the enrollments and funds made available to them through the military services, the Nation's colleges and universities would have slowed down to a virtual halt and would have experienced great difficulty in resuscitating their educational enterprise after the war years.

It is important also to note the practice followed by the Federal Government of permitting advanced students of key sciences to remain in college even during the national emergency. No serious question was raised regarding the practice of draft boards of deferring from active military duty in the name of national defense persons whose training in certain key fields was considered to be of greater value to the defense effort. Thus, Federal policies reached beyond the narrow confines inherent in the earlier illustration of the Military Academy at West Point. Given a Federal need for trained manpower, it was now no longer necessary to provide training on a military post; the definition of military training was extended to include many traditional collegiate studies; and the definition of personnel required to defend the Nation was extended far beyond the reaches of military personnel alone. It all seemed to suggest that, if the emergency were great enough, the boundaries of Federal interest could readily be enlarged to cope with national needs. It indicated, too, that the Nation's institutions of higher education shared with its taxpayers a willingness to serve that national interest.

Indeed, one of the major findings of World War II was the recognition on the part of those responsible for the national defense that highly trained manpower in fields only remotely related (in the popular mind) to the national defense were in fact essential to that national defense. It has been observed that World War II was the "first war in human history to be affected decisively by weapons unknown at the outbreak of hostilities." For the development of such weapons and techniques, much credit had to be given to nonuniformed scientists, drawn largely from the Nation's colleges and universities. Highly skilled personnel, ranging all the way from linguists and cartographers to cryptographers and physicists, mathematicians and biologists, were required to defend the Nation against enemy powers. The defense of the Nation against an enemy being clearly a responsibility of the Federal Government, it required no great argument to persuade the Nation's colleges and universities and the public generally that the Federal Government had a legitimate interest in the training of all persons whose skills bore in any way upon the national defense effort.[7]

The Engineering, Science and Management War Training Program established during World War II is a good case in point. Under this program, Federal funds were paid to colleges and universities to support courses providing critical instruction to civilians. To be sure, it was carefully rationalized on the grounds that it constituted a purchase of services by the Federal Government, but it remains a fact that some $60 million was paid to institutions of higher education, both public and private, for direct operating expenditures. The Engineering, Science and Management War Training Program was promptly discontinued at the end of the national emergency, and it is doubtful that the American people would have elected to continue such a program in peacetime. But constitutions remain in force even during emergencies, and no constitutional question was raised regarding this program.

There is some reason to believe that the war had an additional effect upon educational development in the United States. The practice of the Armed Services of administering to inductees or potential inductees standard national tests of intelligence or achievement, as well as of physical fitness, turned up in World War II, as it had in World War I, appalling statistics on the relative lack of education and training of the Nation's young men. Such discouraging findings lent emphasis to the view that, while education might in the United States be local in control, it was national in implication. The shortcomings of the Nation's schools had, in this instance, a distressing effect upon the Federal Government's ability to defend the Nation. Figures on draft rejections based on inadequate educational training were much in the minds of legislators when they subsequently met to consider postwar educational measures.

Economic Emergencies

Much Federal activity affecting higher education has been the outgrowth of Federal efforts undertaken within the broad context of enumerated general powers. Nowhere has this been better demonstrated than during the period of the "Great Depression." Student assistance made available under the National Youth Administration, construction of physical facilities on public campuses under the Public Works Administration, and loans for construction purposes from the Reconstruction Finance Corporation were all by-products of Federal efforts to provide economic relief to citizens during the Depression under a broad interpretation of its responsibility to promote the general welfare. The only grant assistance made available to *institutions* through Depression-related projects were Public Works Administration grants which were limited to public agencies, as the nature of the legislation made clear. As noted earlier, this is the only instance in United States history when funds declared available to institutions of higher education were limited to public institutions. Here it was simply a matter of public institutions being able to take advantage of their relationship to the States and municipalities that were the intended beneficiaries of the legislation; it was not a case, such as that of the Engineering, Science and Management War Training Program, in which acknowledgment was made of certain sensitivities regarding Federal involvement in education. The net result was not to discourage Federal involvement as such, but only to limit its effectiveness by making it conform to the contours of anticipatable hostilities.

The Depression demonstrated again what wartime emergencies had indicated, namely, that if the American people wanted their Federal Government to act in the field of higher education, it could and would do so. And it could do so legally and constitutionally. On the eve of the Depression, President Hoover's Advisory Commission on Education reported to him that there were 31 provisions of the Constitution under which the Federal Government could find authority for educational actions. President Roosevelt could observe during the Depression that the Constitution ". . . is so simple and practical that it is possible always to meet extraordinary needs by changes in emphasis and arrangement."

Conclusion

If the past is not a guide to the future, awareness of the past is yet a requirement for understanding the present. These brief historical notes do suggest the outlines of some significant patterns in the development of relations between the Federal Government and institutions of higher learning. These would include the following:

1. The Federal Government has long been involved in higher education. There can no longer be any serious dispute over the authority of the Federal Government to enter into activities that may affect directly and intimately the nature, scope, direction, and in some cases the very purposes of higher education. There has been and ought to continue to be dispute and sober consideration over the "how" and "why" of these activities, but the authority to conduct them is not really disputable.

2. Federal involvement in higher education, in the period considered in this chapter, was related to identifiable national needs for personnel or types of training, on the one hand, and to situations involving emergencies, crises, or extraordinary social needs, on the other. To put it the other way around, the Federal Government in this period did not see fit to deal with the problems of higher education itself as an important segment of the society. Rather, it dealt with higher education in terms of what it could contribute directly to other parts or needs of the society, in two instances (the service academies and land-grant colleges) going so far as to call into being new classes of institutions to meet particular needs. Without laboring the point, it should simply be noted that this is a distinction with an important difference, for the approach taken determines in part the ability of institutions to choose their own goals and find their own purposes.

3. As an important corollary of the above, the accepted definitions of national needs, emergencies, and consequently areas of Federal educational concern have broadened over the years. In part, this reflected the growing range of interests and activities within higher education and its increased ability to contribute to the solution of social problems. In part, too, it reflected greater positivism and flexibility within the Federal Government, with an

attendant willingness to mobilize an ever wider range of groups for the solution of national problems.

4. In turning to higher education for help in meeting national needs, the Federal Government has utilized both public and private institutions.[8] If the serious involvement of the Federal Government in higher education is dated from the first Morrill Act, then there has now been one hundred years of experience in which colleges and universities have been treated in a more or less even-handed way by the Government. One hundred years of practice develops precedents and traditions not easily reversed. This particular Federal practice is of key significance in assessing present programs and future prospects.

These four developments, discernible in Federal activities as they grew from Constitutional times until the close of World War II, formed the basis for what followed. In the burgeoning of Federal programs following World War II, these patterns can be seen either extended or modified and as the source of contention either resolved or as yet unreconciled. In a sense, then, what follows in this book is a description and analysis of the growth and maturation of a relationship begun at the birth of the Nation.

NOTES

[1] J. L. Messenger, *Interpretive History of Education,* as quoted by Charles Quattlebaum in "Federal Policies and Practices," *The Federal Government and Higher Education* (Englewood Cliffs, N.J., 1960).

[2] See especially Jefferson's letter to J. Bannister, October 5, 1785.

[3] Jonathan Baldwin Turner envisioned a national institute of science as "the central luminary of the national mind, from which all minor institutions should derive light and heat, and toward which they should also reflect back their own." From his speech at Griggsville, Illinois, May 13, 1850.

[4] It should be noted, however, that a number of private institutions made room on their governing bodies for officers of State government, as though to forestall either charges of indifference or demands for public control.

[5] No attempt has been made here to paint the full picture of higher education in the United States. It is important to note, however, that the pre-land-grant public institutions were constructed largely upon the private model. Their orientation was to the professions and the classical academic foundations thereof, rather than to the concept of preparation for useful employment or the meeting of popular needs. Thus, the Universities of Georgia, North Carolina, and Tennessee have existed from the eighteenth century as an evidence that public support of higher education is not, by definition, support of utilitarian education.

[6] For a summary of the Federal part in the "A and M" movement, see *Land-Grant Colleges and Universities; A Federal-State Partnership,* U.S. Office of Education Bulletin, 1952, No. 21. For a more general treatment of the movement, see E. D. Eddy, *Colleges for Our Land and Time* (New York: Harper & Brothers, 1956).

[7] This interest extended even to regularly enrolled college students, as attested by the operation of the Student War Loan Program, under which some $3.3 million was loaned between 1942 and 1944. Its lending (and collection) experience served, among other things, as an encouraging precedent for the larger, broader, and more generous loan program authorized by the National Defense Education Act of 1958.

[8] It may be relevant to observe that the subvention and use of non-public resources in the national interest were by no means limited to education. The period of American history under discussion is replete with instances of grants to individuals (such as the westward-moving railroads) where an envisioned national interest was to be served.

SIGNIFICANT DATES IN THE RELATIONSHIPS OF THE FEDERAL GOVERNMENT

AND HIGHER EDUCATION

1785	Northwest Ordinance
1787	Contract with The Ohio Company reserving two townships of land for the support of a university
1802	Establishment of U.S. Military Academy at West Point
1819	The Dartmouth College Case
1830	First Federal "research contract" with the Franklin Institute, Philadelphia
1845	Establishment of U.S. Naval Academy at Annapolis
1862	Passage of the Morrill Act
1867	Creation of the Department of Education

Smithson's gift to "found . . . an establishment for the increase and diffusion of knowledge among men"

1874 Award of nautical training grants—first evidence of the principle of Federal "matching grants"

1879 First Federal grants to Howard University

1887 Hatch Act establishing a system of agricultural experiment stations

1890 Passage of the Second Morrill Act

1914 Passage of the Smith-Lever Act for agriculture and home-economics extension

1916 Formation of the National Research Council

1918 Founding of the American Council on Education

1919 First Surplus Property Disposal made to educational institutions

1920 First establishment of ROTC units on college campuses

1931 Hoover's National Advisory Committee on Education report presented

1935 Creation of the National Youth Administration

1937 Public Health Service Fellowships inaugurated

1940 Inauguration of the Engineering, Science and Management War Training Program

Establishment of the National Defense Research Committee (later Office of Scientific Research and Development)

1944 Passage of the Servicemen's Readjustment Act

1946 Establishment of the "Fulbright Program"

First Atomic Energy Commission Fellowship awarded

1946–48 Broadening of Federal Surplus Property Disposal Program

1948 Truman's President's Commission on Higher Education reports

Passage of the Smith-Mundt Act

1950 Supreme Court decides the Texas Law School Segregation Case

Initiation of the College Housing Loan Program

Creation of the National Science Foundation

1951 Initiation of ICA "Contract" Program

1952 First National Science Foundation Fellowships awarded

1953 Second "Hoover Commission" report on education released

1956 Passage of the Health Research Facilities Act

1957 Report of Eisenhower's President's Committee on Education Beyond the High School

1958 USSR Cultural Exchange Agreement announced

Passage of the National Defense Education Act

1961 Creation of Peace Corps

Passage of Fulbright-Hayes Act

Creation of Agency for International Development

CHAPTER TWO

THE POSTURE OF GOVERNMENT

The Setting

If World War I brought America reluctantly into the world, World War II removed any doubt that we were in it to stay. America's new role has entailed the assumption of responsibilities quite without precedent in our history. Every part of our society has been affected by these new responsibilities, and as an integral part of the society, higher education has felt the impact also.

During the war, of course, traditional and normal patterns of behavior had to be put aside with little ceremony. The higher-education community adjusted to the sudden heavy demands put upon it with a readiness that bespoke its patriotism and an ease that belied its reputation for inflexibility and conservatism. Large research programs were mounted on campuses, and many faculty members left the campus to work in Government research installations. Virtually every major scientific and technological advance during the war years bears the imprint of some part of the academic community.

At the same time, the colleges and universities were making major adjustments in curricula that had grown for over a century, in order to undertake special training programs of military personnel. Doctors, dentists, engineers, scientists, language specialists, and many others passed through the campus with a speed that must have been bewildering to those accustomed to the leisurely prewar pace.

With the benefit of twenty years' hindsight, it now seems inevitable that, with such dramatic changes, things could never afterward be quite the same on the campus. Even had it been possible for the world to return in pace and attitude to the prewar era, the events of 1940 to 1945 would have left their imprint.

Such was not possible, of course. New forces were abroad; a new alignment of nations took shape in the world, carrying with it a challenge which, in its magnitude and continuing nature, was altogether new in American history. At home, the Nation faced the problem of what to do with 15 million returning veterans whose lives had been interrupted at a crucial stage and who had to be fitted into the society with skills that would be personally satisfying and socially useful.

Just as the war, then, changed the Nation and higher education, so the postwar period produced further changes. Chief among these changes was the development of a new relationship between the Federal Government and higher education.

It is idle to argue whether the change was a qualitative or quantitative one. Suffice it to say that the contacts between the Federal Government and higher education became more numerous and more complex and involved a great deal more money. They became continuing participants in a network of relationships that has grown each year and shows every sign of continuing to grow.

The most pressing postwar problem involving institutions of higher education was that of training for civilian life veterans returning from the war. The 78th Congress in 1944, in anticipation of the war's end, enacted Public Law 346, the well-known GI Bill.

There are very few events in social life that can truly be called unprecedented. Yet it is accurate to say that the GI Bill had no real precedent in American higher education. This was a social experiment on the grand scale. During its lifetime, Public Law 346 supported almost 2¼ million students in institutions of higher education. An indication of the suddenness of the impact and the magnitude of it can be gleaned from the fact that the total estimated degree-credit enrollment in institutions of higher education in 1939 was 1,365,000. In 1946, enrollment had risen to more than 2 million, and in 1949, the peak year of GI enrollment, it approached 2½ million.

The original GI Bill was followed by another to assist veterans of the Korean War. Under the Korean GI Bill, 1,166,000 students have attended college, bringing the total of students who have attended college with Federal support to almost 3½ million. The results of these massive support programs are not all evident even yet, and some will not be felt for many years. There is now substantial agreement, however, that they were immensely successful. It is clear that the GI Bills both induced and enabled many people to go to college who would otherwise not have done so. The importance to the Nation of a better-educated citizenry is of course obvious. What is perhaps less obvious is that these benefits multiply with each generation, for the children of college-educated parents are more likely, themselves, to go to college.[1]

The GI Bills forged a strong link between the Government and institutions of higher education. Another link, equally strong and perhaps even more significant, has been formed since the end of World War II by the consuming demands of science and technology. A more extensive discussion of the Government's role in sponsoring and purchasing research done in colleges and universities will be found elsewhere in this chapter. It is sufficient at this point to say that the demands of national defense and the exploding progress of science have brought the Federal Government and the higher-education community together in ways and to a degree that would have been unthinkable as little as twenty years ago.

The war and its aftermath, then, produced a new setting for the conduct of higher education—a setting in which the National Government was an element with which to reckon. Putting aside for the moment the effects these circumstances have had on institutions of higher education, it is important first to examine the way in which the Government, on its part, has assumed its new responsibilities.

Further Setting

There can be no true understanding of the ways in which the Federal Government is involved in higher education without an understanding of some basic facts of educational and political life. The facts need not be embraced as good nor rejected as evil, but they must be grasped and comprehended at the outset.

The first of these facts, as we have already seen, is that the Federal Government is "in" higher education on a massive scale—at present more than 15 per cent of the total educational expenditures of the Nation's institutions of higher education comes from Federal sources. Thus, while debate is legitimate, indeed indispensable, on such matters as the nature, purposes, distribution, administration, and effect of Federal programs, there can be no realistic debate about the *fact* of Federal participation.

The Secretary of Health, Education, and Welfare, Abraham A. Ribicoff, made this point strongly when he presented the Administration's higher-education program to a committee of the House of Representatives in March, 1961:

> . . . the question of whether the Federal Government should play a part in the enterprise of higher education is simply not a real one. The Federal Government has had an important part in that enterprise for 100 years. Its part has grown dramatically in the last 20 years, and the real question that faces us . . . is what shall the Federal Government do now, in 1961, to play its part in ways that will contribute to the continued development of a strong and vital system of higher education.

The second fact of importance is that the American Government is not a tidy one. It is doubtful that it ever was, and it is certain that it is not now. The application of this fact to Federal programs in higher education will become evident in the discussion which follows, but some preliminary observations may help to set the stage for that discussion.

The Federal Government has not, obviously, grown in accord with any predetermined plan. In spite of having written and for almost 175 years lived by a Constitution setting out the *scheme* of government, Americans have been indifferent, if not hostile, to the planned development of that government and the society on which it rests. We need not speculate on the causes of this condition, nor should we assume that it has had evil results. If there is no virtue in *un*tidiness, as such, it is equally true that, in social affairs, there is no self-evident virtue in neatness, except to the doctrinaire and the insecure.

A distinctive characteristic of the growth of the Federal Government is that it has grown in response to pressures—pressures from without, such as war and other international tensions, and from within, such as those generated by private-interest groups. The former is obvious, the latter perhaps less so. Nevertheless, it should not surprise us, for we place great importance on our right as individuals to express our views, to join with others who believe as we do, and to take appropriate steps to mold public policy into what we feel to be the proper form.

It is easy to see, then, why the Federal Government often seems to resemble nothing so much as a patchwork quilt; new programs are started, and old ones change direction and emphasis as a complex of influences bear on those responsible for policy making. There is serious doubt whether Americans would prefer it otherwise, but the question is probably irrelevant because there is no doubt that the forces which cause a lack of coherence are strong and sustained.

As a general proposition, the Government is a reflection, if not an image, of the entire society. Its organization and operation in a given area tell us much about the area being served, and conversely, the nature of the constituency involved will be reflected in the way the Government is organized to deal with it. Thus, the third fact central to an appreciation of Government–higher-education relations is that the Federal Government, in the executive or legislative branch, is not organized in any meaningful way to deal with higher education as a whole.

To put this point in a different way, there is a Department of Agriculture to deal with agricultural problems, a Department of Labor to deal with problems in that area, a Department of Commerce to concern itself with problems in the business realm, and so on. However, the only entity in government which deals, on a full-time basis, with higher education is a Division within a Bureau within a Department, and furthermore, that one entity is responsible for but a small fraction of the Government's contacts with higher education.

This is, of course, something of an oversimplification, for many, if not most, questions of public policy cut across such neat jurisdictional lines. In a complex society, public questions are not so easily fitted into boxes; they have a way of frustrating arbitrary methods of classification. Yet even allowing for this, the fact remains that the Government has recognized areas of the society that are identifiable and, as a goal at least, has devised administrative devices to deal with them in a coherent manner. No such attempt has yet been made in the area of higher education.

This is an illuminating fact, for it tells much about the way in which the Federal Government has viewed higher education and about the way the educational community has looked on the Government.

Higher education in the United States is characterized by nothing so much as diversity. It is a vast, sprawling enterprise composed of elements that sometimes seem to have little in common except the fact that they all offer education beyond the high school. It consists of junior colleges, teacher's colleges, liberal arts colleges, institutes of technology, and universities. Part of it is publicly controlled, part private. Its private schools are both sectarian and nonsectarian, and its public schools are controlled by both State and local governments. Far from being a disability, this is claimed—and rightly so—as one of the great strengths of American higher education. We are strong enough, wealthy enough, and vital enough to support the luxury of diversity, and we have turned that luxury into a necessity, into a central value of our society.

Given this condition, it is not at all remarkable that the Government in its program has so far been unable to come to grips, organizationally, with higher education. Indeed, higher education has not yet been able to come to grips with itself, and the disorder in Government reflects this absence of organization in education.

But a further factor is operating to account for the Government's fragmented approach to higher education. The tradition of State, local, and private financing of education is strong among Americans. The belief that education is best served when the responsibility to pay for it rests with the constituency it, in turn, serves is a central part of the American ideology. It has helped to account for the wondrous diversity already noted, and it is tampered with only at great political peril.

Yet it is clear and has been for some time that there is a mythological quality to it, and as with many myths, this one has served to obstruct a clear view of the world. Since World War II, it has been evident that if society is to meet its responsibilities—responsibility for survival as well as progress—it must, through Government action, call on colleges and universities for those things which they alone in our society produce: highly trained manpower and new knowledge.

From the other side, it has become equally clear to many in education that advanced training on the scale and on the level of quality required can be achieved only with the assistance of the taxing powers of the Federal Government.

This awareness has come, it should be said, with some apprehension on both sides. But a mutual self-interest, to the benefit of society at large, has been moving these reluctant lovers into a close and continuing embrace. Neither party, however, is yet willing to admit publicly that the relationship is more than a passing affair. As a result, the Government, on its part, has barely begun to consider seriously the kind of organization needed to deal effectively with higher education on a systematic, long-range basis.

This kind of reluctance to face up to the facts of life is certainly not unique to Government-education affairs. One need only look to the brief history of foreign-assistance programs to see a comparable example in which controlling groups in the body politic have been consistently unwilling to admit the existence of a continuing American commitment. The notion persists that next year we may be able to drop the burden, and so we need not, in fact should not, look beyond next year.[2] There has been a persistent unwillingness until very recently to do anything that would imply a long-range commitment by the Government to higher education. Such an attitude can persist, in the face of facts to the contrary, only with serious risk to the interests of both the Government and institutions of higher education.

CONTEMPORARY PATTERNS: POLICIES AND PROGRAMS

There are many ways in which Federal activities might be described, each valid for a particular purpose. For our purposes—an examination of the scope of Federal programs and an insight into the way the Government is organized to treat with higher education—it is most profitable to look at the subject from the point of view of the broad objects or purposes of Federal programs operated by various Federal agencies.

The Government as Consumer: I. The Demands of Science and Technology [3]

In 1954, American colleges and universities spent on separately budgeted research a total of $409.7 million. This is a rapidly changing world, however, and the need for knowledge of it has gone beyond the simple satisfaction of man's curiosity and become a requirement for his continued existence in it. As a partial measure of this need and the growing awareness of it, this same category of expense leaped by 1958 to a total of $741.3 million.

These totals represent expenditures of three different types. Specifically, $290 million was spent in Federal contract research centers operated by universities but separate from them. In addition, $120 million was spent in agricultural experiment stations, including schools of agriculture. And finally, almost one-third of a billion dollars, $328 million, was spent in universities and colleges proper.

Not all the money thus spent came from Federal sources, of course, but the greater part of it did. To be precise, in the 1958 fiscal year the Government spent $537.8 million in support of research and development in colleges and universities, just over 73 per cent of the total. By 1960 the total Government expenditures for research and development had risen to more than $7.7 billion, of which $453.7 million was spent in educational institutions and an additional $306.3 million in research centers. Research and related activities, then, conducted in or under the auspices of colleges and universities, are virtually dominated financially by the Federal Government and, on the other side, represent the largest area of Federal participation in higher education.

Two important features characterize the greater portion of federally sponsored research. First, it is overwhelmingly directed into the sciences. In 1958, 29 per cent of the total Federal contribution was spent in the engineering fields, 44 per cent in the physical sciences, 23.2 per cent in the life sciences, and 3.3 per cent in the social sciences. In effect, Federal support of research means Federal support of scientific research.[4]

The second feature of Federal programs is that they are primarily mission-oriented; in large part, Federal research funds are spent by agencies with more or less specific missions or purposes. Indeed, only the National Science Foundation, among all Government agencies, has as its mandate the strengthening of *science,* generally, and only the United States Office of Education is charged with serving *education* generally. The sharp focus of Federal programs in research does not necessarily mean, as is often charged, that Federal agencies neglect basic research out of preference for applied research and development. Indeed, just slightly under half of all Federal funds support basic research, and if agricultural research programs and contract research centers are excepted, the figure is closer to 75 per cent. Nevertheless, the focus is significant for what it tells of the kind of relationship which obtains between the higher-education community and the Government in this important area. With some notable exceptions, and at the risk of oversimplification, it is the relationship of buyer to seller—Government agencies buy the services of universities and their faculties in order to carry out the purposes for which the agencies were established. The primary goal of Government agencies is not the promotion of higher education; rather, agencies use the services of institutions of higher education in order to promote their individual goals.

It is in the nature of such a relationship that the buyer will seek out the place at which he can have his work done best. Anything less, in this case, would be a dereliction of duty and a misappropriation of public funds. At the same time, the buyer may well try to develop and encourage new sources of supply, but his chief aim must be to get the best possible product. Thus, Federal research funds are quite unevenly distributed. First, they go overwhelmingly to universities rather than colleges. Kidd says that, in talking about Federal research programs, "university is synonymous with 'institutions of higher education,' since about 95 per cent of all Federal research funds to institutions of higher education go to universities." [5] Furthermore, these funds go to relatively very few universities. In 1953-1954, Federal research funds were granted to 173 institutions. Excluding money spent on contract research centers, 14 of those universities received 55 per cent of the money, and 119 of them received a total of about 5 per cent. Finally, with the exception of agricultural research programs, the Federal money goes in about a 60-40 ratio to private institutions over public.

Clearly, these aspects of Federal research programs have important educational implications, and Government policy makers have become increasingly concerned about them. In the meantime, however, the public business must go on, and in the area of research, it is conducted in a honeycomb of agencies.

Virtually every Government agency is both a producer and a consumer of research; that is, each gets the information it needs partly from its own staff and laboratories and partly from outside sources. Where an agency's chief need is for research of a basic nature relating to its mission, it is more likely to turn to colleges and universities than to any other source. Conversely, as a rough rule of thumb, where its needs are for the development of technology, it is more likely to look to its own resources, to turn to private industry, or to establish separate research centers which may well be run by universities, either singly or in combination.

The Federal agencies conducting the largest research programs involving institutions of higher education are the Department of Agriculture; the Department of Health, Education, and Welfare, which includes the National Institutes of Health and the United States Office of Education; the Department of Defense, including the Departments of the Army, Navy, and Air Force; the Atomic Energy Commission; and the National Science Foundation.

These agencies together account for about 95 per cent of the Federal funds spent in this area. In most important respects they operate independently of each other, with separate statutory mandates and separate, though at times overlapping, missions.

The largest of these contributors is the Department of Defense, which currently accounts for roughly 40 per cent of all Federal research and development funds spent in colleges and universities. In relative terms this share has been declining steadily. In 1952, for example, Defense accounted for about 75 per cent of the Federal funds spent in colleges and universities, exclusive of research centers. Actually, of course, the Defense Department programs have not been shrinking; indeed, they have been slowly growing. Rather, the decade of the 1950s saw a dramatic increase in the programs of the Atomic Energy Commission, the National Institutes of Health, and the National Science Foundation (created in 1950).

It is important to note that the fact that Federal research programs are initiated and conducted with reference to noneducational goals (with the exception of the National Science Foundation) does not necessarily mean that they are in conflict with educational goals. That may or may not be the case, depending on a complex of factors.[6] No one would argue, at this point, that Federal research programs have not strengthened in important ways the research capacity of many universities. Indeed, one university president has said that Government funds have "saved" the research function in higher education. Certainly, in the sciences, with the tremendous expense of scientific research, it is hard to imagine research, in all its present luxuriant growth, without large amounts of Federal support. However, having said this, one must still note the lack of any necessary correspondence between agency purposes and educational needs. Nowhere is this fact better illustrated than in the research programs of the National Institutes of Health.

For the fiscal year 1960, the budget for the research grants programs of the National Institutes of Health amounted to slightly over $200 million. Of all the Federal agencies operating in the area of research, the growth of the National Institutes of Health has been the most dramatic. In 1954 a Division of Research Grants was established to administer a program which totaled, the following year, $780,000. Since that time, institutes have been established with separate research authority under the general direction of the Research Grants Division and the total research budget has leaped more than 200-fold. The years 1948 through 1956 were marked by steady but moderate growth. Suddenly, in 1957, the appropriation for research jumped from $38 million to $93.3 million, and similar increases have occurred in almost every year thereafter.

There can be no doubt about the importance of the mission of this agency or the value of the research it has supported. It is no secret, however, that its programs have grown, not in accord with any systematic notions of the capacity of colleges and universities to absorb increased research loads, nor, on the other hand, of any strong commitment on the part of colleges and universities to focus on the life sciences over other possible choices as an area for research expansion; rather, the growth has been the result of public, and hence strong Congressional, pressures to get about the job of fighting disease as quickly as possible. Indeed, the pattern of the past several years has been for the Congress to increase the appropriation requests of the Administration and for the latter to resist on the ostensible grounds that there is a limit to the amount of money the Nation's research capacity can absorb at one time. The issue is surely arguable, and should be argued, but the point here is that this series of budgetary decisions, which have an important effect on the total programs of colleges and universities, are made each year by agencies with no responsibility and no special competence for judging those effects and that the final decisions bear no necessary relation to any rational picture—if one indeed exists—of what educational institutions, as a whole, ought to be doing.[7]

In one way or another, virtually every Federal research program (again with the partial exception of the National Science Foundation, which encompasses, at least, all the sciences) shares this characteristic. If it be a disability, and we believe that it is, it is not one that is entirely offset by even the wisest administration of these programs, for the point is that there is no place in the decision-making machinery at which judgments of educational priorities can be made before basic decisions on the focus and level of the various programs are finally taken.

At this point it is well to turn to the National Science Foundation, for it plays a central role in the Federal research operation. The National Science Foundation Act of 1950 established the Foundation and authorized it to initiate and support research in the "mathematical, physical, medical, biological, engineering, and other sciences. . . ." In addition, the Foundation was directed "to develop and encourage the pursuit of a national policy for the promotion of basic research and education in the sciences" and "to evaluate scientific research programs undertaken by the agencies of the Federal Government, and to correlate the Foundation's scientific research programs with those undertaken by individuals and by public and private research groups. . . ."

Clearly, a kind of centralizing, or at least coordinating, role was envisaged for the Foundation with regard to Federal policies in basic research, and more broadly with regard to the total national effort.

Certainly, centralization of the Federal effort was not a realistic goal. In the first place, Federal agencies which need to call on the research potential of universities in the fulfillment of their mission will continue to do so, and in doing so, the distinction between basic and applied research, which at best is clear only at the extremes of each category, will more often than not be lost.

In the second place, the virtues of centralization are not at all self-evident, either to scientists or to administrators of institutions of higher education. For both groups the deep-seated American belief in the efficacy of divided power as a safeguard of freedom, both of thought and action, holds powerful sway. On this point the Committee on Institutional Research Policy of the American Council on Education recommended in 1954 that "the Government not concentrate its general purpose research funds in any single Government agency, since such concentration might result in creating a powerful bureaucracy, which could exercise too much control of education and which might lose the great advantages in research management of diversity in method and objective."

Tidiness, as an administrative end in itself, has never had a high priority in the American scheme of things; more than most people, Americans have had a highly sophisticated view of the management of governmental power so as to increase the power of nongovernmental forces.

Centralization, a vain goal, is not the same as coordination, however. It is likely, although not susceptible to proof, that continuing emphasis of the Foundation on basic research and education in the sciences generally has had a salutary, if marginal, effect on Federal research policy. At the very least, it has set, by example, the goal of using the Nation's scientific resources in accord with some conception of a proper distribution of labor among public and private producers of research and has given heed, as part of that goal, to the development of research potential in areas that are not currently in popular demand.

In addition, the very breadth of the Foundation's mandate and its relative freedom to develop new programs to meet newly recognized needs have given it an important leadership role in the Federal research effort. An example here is the Foundation's recently adopted practice of making available to universities, to do with in the scientific fields what they will, an amount equal to 5 per cent of the total research funds granted by the Foundation to each school each year. A variation of this practice has also been adopted by the National Institutes of Health. Some, with a more jaundiced view of human behavior, have suggested that this is in the nature of "conscience money." Whatever interpretation one wishes to give it, there is no doubt that it represents a step in the direction of greater institutional control over its total scientific program. However, at the same time that it moves away from the "project" concept of research support, the new Foundation policy reinforces the maldistribution of the total of research funds. By tying the "free" money to the project money, it ensures that the strong will get even stronger while the weak must scramble for themselves. It is a case of taking a step forward on one front at the expense of a step backward on another.[8]

Such success as the Foundation has had in moderating some of the worst effects of fragmentation has been largely achieved through the power of example rather than direction. Indeed, the Foundation has specifically disavowed even coordination, much less direction, of the Federal research effort as one of its goals. In 1957 the Foundation said:

> The National Science Foundation does not attempt to exercise formal coordinating controls over Federal agencies in the planning or administration of basic research programs. It would be inappropriate to cast the Foundation in the role of critical coordinator of Federal agencies which support basic research. This would be impractical and unrealistic, especially in the case of large agencies because of their strongly mission-related programs.

The Foundation's point of view here no doubt reflects realistically its own place within the Federal power structure. Without a distinctive and influential constituency, and as an independent agency at the subdepartmental level and without cabinet status, it is doubtful that it could exercise formal coordination, even if it wished to.

As in so many other areas of national life, it took an event of dramatic proportions to focus public attention on the existing situation and to jolt the Government into taking action. In this case the event was the launching of the Russian Sputnik and the action was to breathe life into the virtual corpse of an existing group, the President's Science Advisory Committee under the direction of a newly created Special Assistant to the President for Science and Technology. The Committee, in turn, recommended the establishment of a Federal Council on Science and Technology composed of representatives—at the policy-making level—of agencies with important programs in the scientific fields. The purpose of this group is to collaborate on general policy questions rather than to direct the course of Federal science activities or to centralize those activities.

It is the judgment of most informed persons that the new arrangements are an improvement over the old from the Government's point of view. That they may also produce some benefit for higher education is indicated by the report of a special panel under the President's Science Advisory Committee to consider the relationship between research and graduate education. The panel stressed strongly the inseparability of the two, a relationship often lost sight of in the operations of agencies which purchase research on contract.[9]

These new devices for providing policy direction in research are still in their infancy, and it is far too early to assess their net effect. While recognizing their promise for the future, it is still necessary to say that the current judgment on Federal research policies and on the organization of the Government to administer them remains that expressed by Charles Kidd:

> . . . the federal government as a whole has had only very vague research policies and objectives. What the federal government is trying to do is simply the sum of the objectives of the various agencies. But so far as universities are concerned, the total effect of research funds provided by all federal agencies cannot be adequately assessed by looking separately at the effects of each segment. The total volume of federal research funds has repercussions, for example, on the availability of the faculty for teaching, on the funds available for research in the arts and humanities, and on the values and objectives of the faculty and students.[10]

The Government as Consumer: II. Foreign Policy and Higher Education

World War II introduced to the world the idea of total war, war calling for the mobilization of all a Nation's resources and blurring the distinction between civilian and soldier. The aftermath of the war brought a condition with even less precedent—the cold war, a form of war which uses the threat of force, but not force itself; in which the combatants are civilians and not soldiers; and in which any institution in the society might suddenly find itself involved. It is, in short, what someone has called "total diplomacy."

The conduct of diplomacy in whatever guise is, of course, always the responsibility of the central government. In cold-war diplomacy education has become an important weapon and higher education has become an instrument of American foreign policy.

This has been a radical development, both for higher education and for foreign policy. The result was probably predictable. It was summed up by Robert Thayer, former Special Assistant to the Secretary of State for the Coordination of International Educational and Cultural Relations, in a speech at Harvard University:

> One can perhaps find no better example of the rapidity and depth of change that is taking place in the world today than in the phenomenon of . . . our government suddenly being actively plunged into the operational field of education. . . . When something of this kind happens . . . it does not happen in an orderly, logical . . . fashion—it just happens; and almost overnight, seventeen different agencies of the government became engaged . . . in the work of international education. . . . At the present moment [August, 1960] we do not really have an international educational policy.

There are actually more than 17 agencies involved in one way or another in international educational affairs, and at least 13 of them operate programs in which they call on colleges and universities for staff or facilities. The variety of Federal programs in this field is truly wondrous. They range from the well-known Fulbright and Smith-Mundt programs of educational exchange to the establishment of and assistance to the University of the Ryukyus by the Department of Defense.

The latest program to join these ranks is the Peace Corps,

begun in 1961 as one of the first acts of the Kennedy Administration. Within six months of its birth, training programs for Peace Corps volunteers were being conducted on college campuses around the nation, and a flourishing business was in prospect for colleges and universities preparing young men and women for service overseas in activities ranging from road building to the teaching of English as a foreign language. Among the problems faced by this new agency, one is of particular relevance here: Peace Corps officials found that teaching their volunteers some of the more exotic languages they would need was something of a problem because most of the teachers of these languages were already under contract to work in the Language and Area Studies Centers approved by the National Defense Education Act. There is, it seems, a limit on the capacity of institutions of higher education to meet some demands.

These disparate ventures are bound together by a common theme: all of them are educational programs in only secondary or tertiary ways and are something else first of all. The primary objective may be military assistance, economic development, or the promotion of "international understanding," but not the promotion of higher education. This fact has not always been made explicit in the conduct of Federal programs and has therefore been the cause of some confusion, misunderstanding, and even bitterness. In one such case the academic community was aroused at the disclosure that essentially nonacademic and nonscholarly criteria were included in the judgments made in the selection of exchange scholars under the Fulbright Act. Specifically, as a representative of the American Association of University Professors put it, the concern was over "indications that criteria were being applied which did not seem to relate mainly to professional competence and suitability, and the further revelation that apparently there were no procedures by which a judgment based on essentially irrelevant [i.e., political] standards could be adequately challenged by the applicant." The Association further reported that "This criterion is only a point of focus for a pervasive view—the idea that international exchange of scholars is a device for enhancing the reputation of our country and furthering useful general intercourse among nations. . . . What has not been made clear to the American academic world is that these essentially non-scholarly purposes play an important part in both programming and selection."

If there were ever an excuse for failing to apprehend the "essentially non-scholarly purposes" of the educational exchange programs, there is none now, for their primary purpose has been stated with precision and elegance by the individual most responsible for their development, Senator J. William Fulbright. In a speech to the Senate on June 27, 1961, in the course of debate on his bill to codify many of the separate educational and cultural exchange activities, Senator Fulbright made the point in such a way that there can no longer be any doubt. In at least three places in his remarks he explicitly stated the primacy of foreign relations. First, "since there is no question that the exchange programs are primarily designed to bring about mutual understanding among peoples, we are led straight to the conclusion that they are a key factor in our foreign relations." And again, "one result of the sporadic and almost apologetic approach to educational and cultural exchanges has been that we possess no solid legislative base which makes it clear that these programs are an essential part of our foreign relations."

These two statements are clear enough, but the Senator went on to meet directly the conflict between foreign policy and scholarly endeavor. His remarks on the point are worth quoting at some length.

> At this point . . . I would move on from this discussion of the relationship of the exchange programs to our foreign policy. But I must not do so without taking some notice of an argument which has been advanced from time to time by a small minority of individuals in the academic world. . . . This argument, pertaining mainly to Public Law 584 programs, is that the exchanges should have the primary purpose of

advancing pure scholarship on an international basis, and that any foreign policy benefits to the Nation should be regarded as secondary, or even incidental. While I have full sympathy for the desire to promote an international community of scholars unfettered by artificial restrictions, I consider the above argument basically irrelevant.

In the first place, I think it is established beyond question that there is an inevitably close relationship between the exchange programs and our foreign policies. Second, insofar as our official programs are concerned, we must use public funds for purposes of the most immediate and apparent value to the public. A third point has to do with what we mean by the words "education" and "pure scholarship." For my part, I would adhere to a position that emphasizes the quality of humanism, as it is defined in standard dictionaries. Much a matter of controversy as this can be, I nevertheless am very impressed with the following statement by the professor emeritus of literature at Stanford, Albert Guerard:

"The core of a humanistic education is the art of thinking. This art is not purely intellectual; it cannot be reduced to formal logic. It implies a moral attitude; the desire to know the truth, the will to follow the light, the willingness to sacrifice if need be the rugged individualism of immediate self-interest. The center of the humanities is not erudition, even at first hand: it is good will guided by clear thinking. A man who responds to Shakespeare, on the stage or in book form, is nearer salvation than the one who, with icy detachment, has computed the proportion of feminine rhymes in Henry VIII."

My personal belief is that those charged with the actual conduct of the educational exchange program under Public Law 584 have been guided by philosophic ideas not unlike those. The goal of mutual understanding and cooperation has been seen as the end product of the program—not just as an incidental gain.

Whatever one's views on the true nature of humanism, it is evident that there is conflict—in some cases actual and in others potential—between the foreign-policy objectives of the Government and educational objectives of colleges and universities. This conflict could become even greater as the Government calls more and more on higher education to perform services in the international field. The distribution of the present Federal effort is an indication of problems that may be met in the future. The largest Federal expenditures in the foreign field involving colleges and universities are made by the International Cooperation Administration.[11] In the fiscal year 1960 the International Cooperation Administration spent about $20 million (exclusive of overhead costs) on university overseas contracts. About 100 contracts were in force with about 50 institutions. Under these contracts American universities undertake to provide assistance to foreign countries in developing their own educational institutions, or parts of them that are of particular importance to the technical-assistance program in each country. In addition, ICA spent $10 million on training individuals from overseas in American institutions. This training must be directly related to specific technical projects in the country, and foreign nationals so trained rarely earn degrees.

The mission of ICA is to promote the economic development of beneficiary nations, and education is but one function of this mission. Recognizing this, the ICA programs involving education are largely parceled out for administration to the Government agencies having special competence, e.g., the Department of Agriculture, the National Science Foundation, and the United States Office of Education. Policy and budgetary control, however, are largely retained by ICA. Thus, the International Cooperation Administration's education money contributes to the same fragmentation observed in domestic education programs.

In general, ICA activities in education suffer from the devil that has plagued the foreign-assistance programs from their start, namely, Congressional unwillingness to make any long-term commitment to the idea of foreign aid. If this is troublesome in the building of roads and bridges, which takes several years to accomplish, it can be fatal in the development of educational institutions and of trained manpower, both of which are considerably longer-term propositions.

The framework and scheme of operations in the field of economic assistance prior to 1962 did not give much hope for the wise use of educational resources in overseas economic development. The Act for International Development of 1961 gave hope for improvement, however. First, as already noted, it contained five-year authorization for development loans. Second, the legislation which authorized the new Agency for International Development contained the following direction: "In providing technical assistance under this Act in the field of education, health, or housing the head of any such agency shall utilize, to the fullest extent practicable, the facilities and resources of the Federal agency or agencies with primary responsibilities for domestic programs in such field."

While the provision is obviously not self-executing, its sponsor, Senator Hubert Humphrey, stated its purpose in the field of education as "giving the U.S. Office of Education a mandate to do more of what it is capable of doing in international education." More specifically, he said:

> The Office of Education should be given substantial responsibilities in operating those parts of international education programs which function inside the United States. The Office of Education should aid in the recruitment of personnel and should provide other advice and services to those programs which are operated by other branches of the Federal Government. And finally, the professional resources of the Office of Education should be available to any other part of the Government for the review of the effectiveness of any of their educational programs.

It is yet too early to know what, if any, difference all of this will make in actual practice. The Humphrey amendment, though, bespeaks an awareness of the problem and a determination to provide a sounder basis for educational activities conducted in the context of economic development.

The second major participant in foreign educational ventures is the Department of State. In fiscal year 1960, the State Department spent $15 million on its various exchange programs. In spite of the conflict of goals mentioned earlier, the exchange programs have been warmly received in the educational world. The benefits that accrue to individuals and their institutions from the opportunity to teach, study, or conduct research abroad are obvious and welcome. Most institutions also welcome the opportunity to have foreign students and faculty on their campuses. The problems here, however, particularly with students, have from time to time caused institutions a good deal of anguish. In general, the problems center around the lack of preparation for college work of many exchange students, especially those from underdeveloped nations, and the lack of care sometimes evident in directing students to the schools which can best serve them. Both of these problems will become more vexing in the future as the exchange programs bring an increasing number of undergraduate students and as they shift focus to include more students from the emerging African nations.

The State Department, like ICA, has largely delegated the operating responsibilities for its programs to other agencies. Unlike ICA, it uses nongovernment as well as Government agencies. For example, the Institute of International Education administers the Fulbright and Smith-Mundt programs for graduate-student exchange; exchange of teachers and school administrators is arranged by the U.S. Office of Education; and the Conference Board of Associated Research Councils arranges for the exchange of professors.

There is general agreement that neither the State Department nor the International Cooperation Administration can be effective agents for the conduct of educational programs. It is equally clear, however, that the conduct of foreign policy will increasingly involve the use of educational resources. Moreover, even greater attention is being focused on the international aspects of education. On the one hand, this attention takes the form of serious studies of the subject, such as the one conducted under the auspices of the Ford Foundation by a Committee headed by President Emeritus L. M. Morrill of the University of Minnesota. On the other, it is shown by the brief flurry of charges and countercharges in 1960 between then Senator John F. Kennedy and various Republicans over a grant by the Joseph P. Kennedy Foundation to bring to this country a number of African students, after the State Department had declined to support the venture.

In addition, there is increasing restiveness in the Congress over the lack of order in present programs. In 1959, a subcommittee of the Government Operations Committee of the House of Representatives reported:

> Although some informal and irregular interagency relationships exist, no single executive or legislative agency, office or committee has an overall responsibility for the coordination of these programs. There is a formal arrangement for coordinating and avoidance of duplication of efforts of two programs—the international educational exchange program of the Department of State and the technical assistance program of the International Cooperation Administration. There is, however, no such arrangement respecting the administration of all the other programs of the Government in this field; and there is in fact no overall coordination of these activities. . . . With policy and administrative detail being handled and personnel to participate being selected by different agencies, the question of overlapping and duplication becomes an important one.
>
> It seems clear that there is not only the lack of overall policy and the lack of an overall coordinating agency but there has been even a lack of comprehensive, organized information on what all the agencies of the Government are doing in this field.

The activities of the Government in international education are perhaps best described as being in a state of flux. Their organization is seriously questioned, and their goals have yet to be even minimally defined. In this area, even more than in the area of research, the clarification of goals is of great importance to higher education. Since research is and always has been a major part of the mission of higher education, institutions are better able to absorb Government demands and to assess and articulate their own needs. However imperfectly this has been done until now, it is a task well within the ability of the institutions.

Such is not the case in the international field, for the Government is asking universities to assume functions that are, in significant measure, outside the traditional stream of educational activity. It is doubly important, therefore, for the Government to make a genuine effort to state clearly the purposes for which it needs to use institutions of higher education and to study carefully the ways in which they may be best used.[12] Equally important is the recognition that there is a sense in which institutions cannot and must not "be used", a sense in which they are effective only when they are freely serving their own values. It will then be necessary for each institution to judge its own best contribution in the light of its own goals. At this point it is evident that thorny problems lie ahead for both sides.

The Government and Trained Manpower: I. Support of Students

From the foregoing it is clear that institutions of higher education perform services that are of immense value to the Government and that a variety of programs exist which, in one way or another, draw on those services. A second dimension of Federal activity in higher education stems from the growing awareness that a Nation's people are its prime natural resource and that in the world today a level of skill and education is required for those people that was unthought of fifty years ago. To say this, however, may suggest a degree of rationality and clarity of goals in the Government's efforts in the manpower field that simply does not exist.

In the area of student support in higher education the one statement that can be made with confidence is that, excepting the GI Bills, which had their genesis in essentially noneducational factors, until the passage of the National Defense Education Act, student support programs were directed almost exclusively toward the graduate level and were largely coordinate with, if not direct by-products of, research programs. This is not to say that they were insignificant. To the contrary, Federal support of students in graduate schools has been one of the major developments in the postwar history of American education.

Federal funds are used to support college study in three ways: by fellowships, by loans, and by pay for work performed on sponsored research. The last of these is by far the most difficult to assess accurately because the sponsoring agencies themselves have no way of knowing precisely how many students work on projects they support and how much they are paid. However, it is estimated that something between 20,000 and 30,000 graduate students are earning money by working on federally sponsored research projects and that the total sum involved is in the neighborhood of $40 million a year. If these figures are approximately correct, then the Government by this hidden subsidy is supporting several times as many graduate students as are helped by the direct fellowship method.

Obviously, every agency that distributes funds for research is at the same time conducting a student-aid program. Furthermore, the correlation between research and graduate education is so close that this is an inevitable by-product of any research support program. However, so dispersed are the sources of these funds and so disparate are the objectives of the agencies administering them that it is extremely difficult to get a coherent picture of the effects of this substantial student-aid program and the ways in which they fit, or fail to fit, into outright support programs and into the higher-education system as a whole. Three things, however, can be said with some confidence.

First, this form of student assistance goes overwhelmingly to those in the sciences. Kidd estimates that about half of the research assistants are employed in the physical sciences, 25 per cent in the life sciences, and 20 per cent in engineering. That leaves 5 per cent for all nonscience fields. Second, since research assistantships accompany grants and contracts, they tend overwhelmingly to be concentrated in a relatively few institutions. This form of bounty tends, along with other forces, to attract the best students to these institutions or, conversely, to make it difficult for other institutions to attract high-quality students. Finally, there is little doubt that the availability of this money has made it more difficult for institutions of all kinds to find high-quality graduate students for teaching assistantships. Just how serious this problem is, is a matter of some dispute, but there is general agreement that the attractiveness of the opportunity to help a senior scholar with his research and the generally higher stipends for research assistants have tended to leave undergraduate teaching assignments to lower-quality graduate students.

Federal programs involving direct aid to students were, prior to the passage of the National Defense Education Act, limited to graduate students. Furthermore, they were directed almost exclusively into the scientific fields. The major programs were operated by the National Science Foundation and the National Institutes of Health.[13] In the fiscal year 1961, the latter awarded about 1,100 predoctoral fellowships, and the former awarded more than 2,100 in its Graduate and Cooperative Graduate programs.

The limitations on these programs in terms of fields of study and level of students supported are accounted for by the fact that the Government until September, 1958, had nothing that approached a consistent philosophy of student financial assistance. By inference from the existing pattern, one can say, of course, that such a philosophy did exist. If so, that philosophy in sum was that financial assistance ought to be given only to students who have made reasonably clear professional commitments to careers in which trained people are deemed to be in short supply and in which the training of additional people is judged to be in the national interest. Another aspect of this philosophy is that in organizational terms the administration of, and policy responsibility for, such programs as do exist should be given to the agencies whose particular goals are closest to the subject fields deemed worthy of support.[14]

Viewed against this backdrop, the National Defense Education Act represented a major shift in the Government's attitude toward student financial assistance. It is important to note that the National Defense Education Act was an addition to, and not a substitute for, existing programs. Its significance, however, is not diminished by that fact. In brief, the National Defense Education Act represents the first major step toward the positive position that the national well-being requires that every individual have an opportunity for the most advanced training of which he is capable. Although the concrete measures embodied in the Act fall short of fulfilling its philosophical commitment, it is worth examining more closely the nature of that commitment and the measures enacted thus far to meet it.

Title I of the Act is devoted to a declaration of policy. It says in part:

> The Congress hereby finds and declares that the security of the Nation requires the fullest development of the mental resources and technical skills of its young men and women. The present emergency demands that additional and more adequate educational opportunities be made available.
>
> We must increase our efforts to identify and educate more of the talent of our Nation. *This requires programs that will give assurance that no student of ability will be denied an opportunity for higher education because of financial need. . . .*
>
> To meet the present educational emergency requires additional effort at all levels of government. It is therefore the purpose of this Act to provide substantial assistance in various forms

to individuals, and to States and their subdivisions, in order to insure trained manpower of sufficient quality and quantity to meet the national defense needs of the United States.

Even accepting the use of the term "national defense" at its face value, this statement stands as a firm declaration of a broad principle that is at least 90 degrees and closer to 180 degrees from previous Government policy. One of America's great social contributions to the world has been a workable system of public education open to all citizens. Under State authority this system has been carried forward by means of State colleges and universities. But the Congress of the United States had never before declared that it was a goal of *national* policy that "no student of ability will be denied an opportunity for higher education because of financial need."

It is a natural temptation to make more of such broad declarations than is warranted by the facts. Nevertheless, while the facts of the National Defense Education Act do not meet its stated objectives, they do introduce several elements that are genuine departures from traditional Government policy. Not the least of these is that the Act vests responsibility for administration of its programs in the United States Office of Education rather than, as might well have happened, in a newly created agency or in an existing agency with narrower goals. Thus, for the first time, the only Government agency whose purview includes all education was given responsibility for important programs whose effects reach all education.

Second, the two major student-assistance programs in the Act, the Student Loan and Graduate Fellowship programs, are potentially available to students in all fields of study; the latter is noncategorical in its coverage, while the former extends "special consideration" to students with a superior academic background who express a desire to teach in elementary or secondary schools and students whose background indicates a superior capacity or preparation in science, mathematics, engineering, or a modern foreign language. In practice, students in all fields and at all levels are eligible to apply and to be granted loans.

The Act provides for the establishment of Loan Funds at participating institutions—some 1,400—with each Federal contribution of $9 to be matched by $1 of institutional funds. All authority for making loans, as well as the responsibility for collecting them, rests with the institutions. By June 30, 1961, more than $130 million had been loaned to over 200,000 students, who borrowed an average of $450 each.

The Student Loan Program served in the National Defense Education Act as a substitute for an outright scholarship program which failed at the last minute to generate enough legislative support. It is not at all clear, even yet, the extent to which loans fill the same needs as would scholarships, or, for that matter, just what the long-range economic and social consequences are of encouraging large numbers of college students to incur sizable debts in pursuit of their education. Two things are clear, however. One is that the Federal Government has taken a long step toward a large-scale, continuing effort to ensure a college education to all able students. The other is that a Federal action, largely unforeseen by institutions of higher education, has brought about a significant shift in the entire pattern of financing a college education. For better or for worse—and there are arguments to support both —widespread borrowing to meet the costs of college is an accomplished fact. This is the kind of development that, once established, is hard to reverse.

The Graduate Fellowship Program, the other major student-assistance program embodied in the Act, is different from other Government fellowship programs in three significant ways. First, it has already been mentioned that students in all fields of study may be awarded fellowships. The only priority set is in terms of career goal—a preference is given to students who are considering teaching in institutions of higher education. Thus, it is the only Federal student-aid program directed toward a problem common to all parts of the higher-education community, the shortage, actual and prospective, of well-qualified teachers. By 1961, 4,000 fellowships had been awarded under this part of the Act; 26 per cent went to students in the humanities, 6 per cent in education, 29 per cent in the social sciences, 12 per cent in the biological sciences, 19 per cent in the physical sciences, and 8 per cent in engineering.

Two actions taken by the Congress in 1961 cast some doubt on the future of this aspect of the Fellowship Program. Indeed, the Fellowship Program is an illuminating example of the outer limits of Congressional willingness to support higher education in all of its aspects. In response to criticism from some members of Congress and some parts of the public, the fiscal year 1962 appropriation for the Fellowship Program contained language prohibiting the Commissioner of Education from awarding any fellowships unless he finds that the awards are consistent with the overall objective of the NDEA to "insure trained manpower of sufficient quality and quantity to meet the national defense needs of the United States." At issue here were fellowships that had been awarded in such fields as folklore, drama, music, and religion.

Even more pointed than the appropriations action was a warning contained in the Report of the Senate Committee on Labor and Public Welfare on proposed amendment to NDEA. The Committee recommended prohibiting any awards in the field of religion and limiting the awards generally to "such subjects as the Commissioner finds are important to the national defense." The Committee went on to say:

> In thus restricting the Commissioner of Education, the committee does not intend to imply that only a very narrow selection of courses is related to the strength of the Nation. On the contrary, the committee believes that the strength of the Nation rests significantly upon overall excellence in college and university faculties in the humanities and social sciences, as well as in science, mathematics, engineering, and modern foreign

languages. Indeed, a well-educated scientist or linguist is in need of exposure to excellent instruction in fields other than his specialty. However, the committee believes that, in the light of the general objectives of this act, expenditures should be concentrated in those fields of study—sciences, engineering, humanities, and social sciences—which are closest to the defense needs of the Nation. The preparation of college teachers in history, economics, government, for example, is more directly related to a strong system of undergraduate training to meet the nation's defense manpower needs, than are graduate programs in folklore or church music.

In the case of the NDEA Fellowship Program, the Congress seems to have drawn back from its presumed position of 1958 that all fields of study are of some significance to the strength of the Nation, and adopted instead the Orwellian position that all fields are equal, but some are more equal than others.[15]

Second, the provisions of the Act require the Commissioner of Education to promote the widespread geographical distribution of the facilities for graduate study in deciding which graduate programs will have fellowships allotted to them. The significance of this feature of the Act is evident in the light of the strong tendency of Federal funds, including other fellowship awards, to pile up at a relatively few institutions. For example, out of a total of 259 students studying physics in 1959 with the help of the National Science Foundation Graduate Fellowships, 157, or about 60 per cent, were enrolled at 5 institutions: Harvard, the California Institute of Technology, Princeton, the Massachusetts Institute of Technology, and the University of California. The remaining 40 per cent were spread among 34 institutions. Similar situations obtained in other disciplines.

From the point of view of the Foundation and its goal of strengthening the sciences, there is every reason why the best students, as chosen in a national competition, should go to the universities with the strongest science faculties and facilities. Yet, as a matter of educational policy, someone must ask and answer the question of whether there are enough of the "strongest" institutions to do the training job that needs to be done.[16] In quantitative terms, the question is whether it is the wisest distribution of educational resources that has 10 institutions awarding 35 per cent of the doctors' degrees each year. The significance of the National Defense Graduate Fellowship Program is that it represents a Congressional answer to that question, and the answer is negative. The Congress called for the development of new facilities in graduate education and for those facilities to be spread over a broader geographic base.

The political appeal of such a policy is obvious; the educational soundness is by no means unanimously acclaimed, with the opposition led, as might be expected, by some of the largest and best institutions in the country. The vigor with which opposing points of view have been presented on this issue has had a healthy effect on Federal policy, for it has put competing needs and interests more sharply into focus, and on institutions, for it has made institutions of all types examine more clearly their own roles in broader perspective.[17]

Most important, however, is the fact that the Government, through this program and through the Student Loan Program, has expressed, in the most systematic terms yet, a national policy for one part of higher education and has set out means to reach the policy goal. There are situations in which any policy is better than no policy, because the existence of a defined position helps to crystallize alternatives. This is one of those situations. The absence of any coherent Federal policy regarding student assistance and the Federal responsibility for it had led to drift and an unfortunate confusion of purposes. The National Defense Education Act programs have provided a point from which further debate over ends and the means for reaching them can proceed.

The Government and Trained Manpower: II. Teacher Competence

A larger and growing aspect of Federal activity is the variety of programs whose purpose is the upgrading of teaching competence, ranging from elementary school through college. In pursuing this purpose, Government agencies make grants or enter into contracts with institutions of higher education for the conduct of institutes which bring teachers back to school for a summer, a semester, or a full academic year.

As might be expected, the administration of these institutes varies according to the subject-matter field involved. The National Science Foundation offers a program of institutes which includes summer institutes for elementary school, secondary school, and college-level teachers in science and mathematics, academic year institutes for secondary school teachers, and in-service institutes for parttime training. All except the last provide a stipend for attendance. The Office of Education, under the National Defense Education Act, offers a program of summer, semester, and academic-year institutes in counseling and guidance and modern-foreign-language teaching. Public school teachers attending these institutes also receive a stipend.

The increasing use of the institute device as a means of improving teacher quality is a particularly interesting but little noted development in Federal policy. Like so many other aspects of Federal policy in education, it seems simply to have grown up quietly while no one was paying much attention. But a substantial amount of money is involved—in the fiscal year 1961, about $7 million went for the language institutes, $6.5 million for those in guidance and counseling, and more than $30 million for the ones operated by the National Science Foundation.

From the standpoint of the Federal Government, two features of these programs are of special significance. First, the institutes constitute what might be called an "integrated" scheme of training;

that is to say, the Government pays an institution for the cost of operating an institute, including faculty salaries, books, laboratory equipment, and overhead costs, and in addition pays stipends to those attending the institute. The only other Government operation comparable with this is the Training Grants Program of the National Institutes of Health, but grants under that Program are more in the nature of subsidies for the conduct of particular training programs than full-cost payments.

The second element of interest in the institutes program is that they represent a sidewise approach to a problem that the Government has not seen fit to approach frontally; that is, the general problem of teacher qualifications. Perhaps it would be fairer to say that, through the various institutes programs, the Government has acknowledged one aspect of the problem, namely, the improvement of the existing corps of teachers, while leaving untouched what is at least equally important, namely, the basic education and training of people who are studying to be teachers.

It is worth noting that a characteristic of many Federal programs is their tendency to approach an objective by indirection or to aim at the periphery rather than the center of the problem. The reasons for this in any given case may be quite legitimate, even compelling. Indeed, in some cases it may have been necessary to choose between something less than ideal and nothing at all—not an uncommon choice in political affairs. The difficulty is that what was originally recognized as being imperfect or incomplete develops in time momentum of its own; its existence is rationalized to the point where the original imperfections are quite forgotten, if only because those involved in the program—on both sides—have a stake in having them forgotten. Thus, the existence of an imperfect solution to a problem becomes a justification for failing to seek a more perfect one.

Lest this seem altogether too abstract, it should be pointed out that there is now great interest in extending the institute method to embrace the teaching of social studies and English. By itself, this is an encouraging development, for if there are to be institutes to improve teaching quality, it would be marked progress for the Government to recognize the problem in the social and humanistic part of the curriculum. There is little doubt that there is room for considerable improvement in the teaching of those subjects and that one way of getting that improvement is to upgrade the knowledge and skill of present teachers. There is *no* doubt, however, that this is but a partial solution and that the root of the problem—that part of it, at least, that is within the scope of higher education— lies in the way teachers are educated in college. Perhaps this is not an appropriate area of governmental interest. That is at least arguable. The danger is that, given the way Federal policy is made, the existence of a partial palliative may inhibit, if not suppress altogether, discussion of basic remedies.[18]

The Government and Trained Manpower: III. Officer Training

In most aspects the Government as employer stands in no different relationship to higher education than does any other large employer; that is, it competes in the market for the best people it can get. In the special area of the Armed Services, however, the Government has traditionally had a preferred position in its efforts to build a competent corps of officers, both for the career service and the reserve forces. The principal mechanism through which this position is maintained is the Reserve Officers' Training Corps —a program of military training incorporated into the regular college curriculum which leads to an officer's commission in one of the services upon completion of the program and graduation from college. In some cases students receive financial support for their education in return for their ROTC commitment; in others, the inducement of an officer's commission is sufficient lure.

Historically, the ROTC program has centered in the land-grant colleges and universities, since the first Morrill Act required that the new land-grant institutions offer instruction in military tactics.

From this start 313 institutions now have an ROTC program for at least one of the services and 177 require ROTC training for all male students in their freshman and sophomore years. Obviously, this is a program of considerable magnitude for colleges and universities.

It is of great importance to the Armed Services as well. The Department of Defense has estimated that the annual requirement for ROTC graduates for the next 10 years will be 14,000 for the Army, 3,000 for the Navy, and 4,000 for the Air Force. These figures should be judged against the fact that the annual graduating class of the U.S. Military Academy is 550 to 600, and that of the U.S. Naval Academy about 900.

ROTC is an expensive proposition, and it is probably more expensive for the institutions than for the Government. For example, in a recent year the Navy spent $8,670,000 for the operation of the Naval Academy, which enrolled 3,700 midshipmen that year. In the same year, the Navy spent $4 million for its so-called "regular" ROTC program, a contract arrangement which provides support for the student in exchange for four years of active service after graduation. This program had 6,200 participants in school during that year.

Actually, the services provide the staff and equipment for the military courses, while each institution provides space and, of course, the regular academic training for the student. That the presence of an ROTC program represents a financial drain on the host institution is not denied by anyone. The precise nature and extent of the drain is in dispute, however, as well as the best means for stopping it. In "normal" times a dispute of this nature might well be only a minor annoyance to the parties to it. The problem is magnified, however, as institutions find themselves with their hands full trying to accommodate the swelling number of students seeking admission. Increasingly, educators have come to believe that they should not be asked to provide space and devote other resources without adequate recompense for what is, after all, the most distinctively Federal function of all—the maintenance of the military establishment.

This attitude lies behind the growing pressures for the abolition of compulsory college ROTC—a trend that is gaining momentum. Officials of the Defense Department have indicated that they do not believe that compulsory ROTC is necessary in order to maintain military strength, but there is evidence of controversy within the Department about the soundness of this view. The Department of the Army in particular, as the largest beneficiary of compulsory ROTC, has been reluctant to part with it.

The resolution of the conflict over who should pay for ROTC programs is still in the bargaining stage. Proposals range from grants for buildings and other facilities, favored by many institutions, to a "bounty" for each ROTC graduate commissioned, favored by many Government officials. The issue is being brought to a head, however, by the growing economic pressures on institutions in the performance of their regular functions, and a full recognition of the magnitude of these pressures by responsible Government officials will be necessary for a satisfactory resolution. As one university head has said, "The failure of the Defense Department to face up to the needs of the institutions has created a situation whose impact neither party to the dispute can now well define." [19]

Aid to Institutions: Concern for the Producer

One way to describe the Government's posture toward higher education—perhaps a charitable way—is to say that the Government has been selective in its approach. Each of the programs so far described touches upon a particular part of higher education—a part of the curriculum, or a part of a faculty member's total job, or some other single aspect of an institution's entire mission. Almost without exception they are specific programs for particular purposes.

What of the producer, however? Is there a danger that, amid

the welter of special services institutions are asked to provide and the individual programs in support of isolated institutional functions, the institution as a whole will be lost sight of? Has the Government, in its dealings with higher education, exercised the prudence expected of an intelligent user of a national resource to ensure that it is not depleted? [20]

Increasingly, the answer from responsible college and university officials is that there is real danger of damage to higher education as a whole. There is, for example, a growing belief among some people in higher education that Federal programs in aid of students ought to be resisted until help is forthcoming for the facilities needed to handle the students. A spokesman for this point of view, President David D. Henry of the University of Illinois, said, following passage of the National Defense Education Act:

> In the absence of a plan and in the confusion over what ought to be done, Congress has taken both limited and disappointing action. . . . These sums were appropriated to help students go to college at a time when unprecedented enrollments are already in prospect. Further, these actions were taken when there were before the Congress important measures to help the colleges handle the new numbers. The bills for loans for college housing, for payment for ROTC facilities, for administrative costs in public health research are examples of the ways the Federal Government could appropriately have helped institutions and which should have had priority over the new appropriations which were authorized.[21]

The question of assigning priorities among competing needs is, of course, what policy making is really about. That such questions are so often resolved on the basis of what is most possible rather than what is most desirable does not remove the necessity for discussion of the priorities. Since these matters are never finally resolved and are perennially debated, it should be reported in preparation for the next round that the Federal Government has done little that was not directed toward a particular goal outside of higher education itself. To put it another way, the Government has made but a limited contribution toward enabling institutions of higher education to meet the broader social and intellectual responsibilities that are uniquely theirs and of which the limited Government programs are but a part.

There are several programs aimed generally at assisting higher education, and it is worth looking at them briefly now. The most important of them is the College Housing Loan Program. This Program, authorized in 1950 but delayed in starting because of the Korean War, has so far loaned to colleges and universities a total of some $2 billion. The loans may be used for the construction of dormitories or other revenue-producing facilities. They are to be repaid over a period of up to fifty years at a rate of interest equal to the average annual rate which the Government pays on all public debt obligations plus ¼ per cent. This can mean a difference of as much as 2 per cent lower interest than if the money were borrowed from private sources.

In establishing this program, the Congress, probably to avoid the controversy that inevitably surrounds an *aid-to-education bill,* decided to treat it as being essentially a noneducational matter and placed the responsibility for its administration in the Housing and Home Finance Administration. The law gives the Administrator of HHFA the authority to consult with the Commissioner of Education and to secure his advice and recommendations. Such consultation does in fact take place, but the final decision on the making of all loans resides with the Administrator of the housing agency.

Leaving aside for the moment the political considerations involved, there is serious doubt about the wisdom of such an administrative arrangement. It would seem to be a reversal of priorities that puts authority with the technical specialists, who then seek advice on educational policy from the agency competent to make the judgments. This should not be taken to mean that people in higher education are necessarily unhappy about the present arrangement. On the contrary, they are pleased with it. As we have noted elsewhere, educators have traditionally been reluctant to see too much authority in any single agency and ask only, when the problem concerns them, for coordination rather than centralization.[22] In any event, administrative theory is less important than proven results, and the College Housing Loan Program, it is generally agreed, has been a huge success. Its major defect, from the point of view of the academic community, has been only that it is too narrow to do the job that needs to be done.

The job that needs to be done is a truly impressive one, and if the Government is to assist in it—as it most likely will—the organizational problem will assume greater importance than it has had heretofore. It seems fairly clear that, in the near future, the Government will undertake to help colleges and universities in the sizable job of capital expansion that lies immediately ahead. Any business that can predict a doubling of the demand for its product within 10 years is likely to find itself in the market for new capital to provide the means for increasing production. It is well known that colleges and universities expect enrollments to double in the 1960s, and it is estimated that some $20 billion will be needed in the 1960s for the capital replacement and expansion to meet that swelling demand.

Clearly, loans for dormitories and other revenue-producing facilities help but little to build the classrooms, laboratories, and libraries that will be needed. Indeed, it is doubtful whether the loan technique itself, even if extended to embrace academic facilities, is suitable for those non-revenue-producing items.[23] Whatever means are chosen to meet the problem, however, both Government and higher education may well have to face up to the question of whether it is wise public or academic policy to have the entire academic building program vested in the Housing Agency; whether the College Housing Program and the academic-facilities program should be operated by two separate agencies—perhaps the U.S. Office of Education for the latter; or whether the housing program should be taken from HHFA and combined with the academic-facilities programs in the other agency. Each of these alternatives involves painful political, bureaucratic, and educational problems. The choice that is ultimately made, however, particularly if it should be the last of the three, could stamp for many years to come the organization of the Federal Government for higher education.

Also in the area of aid for physical facilities, although quite specialized, is the Health Research Facilities Program operated by the Public Health Service. Virtually every medical school in the country and many hospitals participate in this Program, which has provided $30 million a year since 1957 on a 50–50 matching basis for use in building or equipping new facilities for the conduct of health research. There was a bill before the 87th Congress, sponsored by the Administration, to provide 50–50 matching grants for the construction of teaching facilities in the medical field, as well as scholarships for medical and dental students. While no action was taken on the proposal, this too is a likely area for legislative action in the near future.

In sum, the few Federal programs that offer assistance for improving or expanding college and university physical plants have so far made important but tangential contributions toward meeting plant needs. No substantial thrust has yet been made toward meeting one of the most serious needs: the construction of buildings such as classrooms, offices, and teaching laboratories that do not produce income and hence are not in any real way self-liquidating. Furthermore, it seems clear that if this need is to be met in the future, the organizational arrangement of present programs will not be adequate.

The only other significant Federal program directly in aid of institutions of higher education is, of course, the Land-Grant College Act. Under it, and the various additions to it, a total of $5,051,500 has been distributed by formula to the States in every year since 1952. (A distribution has been made in every year since 1890, but in smaller amounts.) The 86th Congress, recognizing increased costs stemming from inflation and growing enrollments, authorized an increase in the total to over $14 million.

To illustrate the unpredictable nature of governmental organization, it should be noted that these funds, alone of all the programs touching the Land-Grant schools as a group, are administered by the U.S. Office of Education, while the rest of the programs directed specifically at those institutions are operated by the Department of Agriculture.

Other programs, including those discussed here in different contexts, can no doubt legitimately be thought of as "aid" to institutions. Any classification, after all, must at some points be arbitrary, and the degree of arbitrariness will increase in proportion to the complexity of the objects being classified. Still, the conclusion is inescapable that the Federal Government has been primarily concerned with the services higher education can perform and only incidentally with the long-run strength and vitality of higher education per se.

Some reasons for this condition may be inferred from what has already been said; others will emerge from the discussion which will follow of the political, ideological, and educational issues that are a part of any proposal for Federal educational activity. We take note, however, of the condition itself.

It should be said that an exhaustive canvass and analysis of the full range of Federal activities affecting higher education would fill a volume in itself. For our purposes, however, such a survey is not necessary. The essential points come through clearly with but a light sketch of the outline of these activities. The growth of Federal programs, measured by dollars or the number of points of contact with institutions of higher education, or any other measure one might choose, has been luxuriant. In general, the growth has been by addition rather than integration; that is to say, as a new area of need has been identified, a new program has been added; or, to mention the other part of the process, as another agency has found it necessary to turn to universities to fulfill its objectives, it has simply done so. The result has been a tropical hothouse of programs, each run with little attention to the other and each encompassing a more or less isolated part of the academic spectrum. The whole, when it can be viewed as a whole, represents something less than—or at least different from—a broad-scale program of assistance to higher education.

It should be clear by now, however, that Federal policy toward higher education is not made in the abstract. Perhaps more accurately, it may be conceived in the abstract, but the baby, when it is born, shows the unmistakable imprint of the facts of bureaucratic, political, and educational life. It should be reemphasized that this casts no reflection on the administration of any single program, nor indeed on its justification. In general, existing programs are both filling a real need and are administered with a high degree of competence. What is in question is the system as a whole and whether it is well designed to meet the needs of higher education as a whole. This is a far more important question, for if the manner in which the Government is organized to deal with higher education is seriously defective, then future Federal effort, no matter how well intentioned, can only add confusion to disarray.

THE BIG PICTURE: CONGRESS, COMMITTEES, AND COMMISSIONS

It can be argued with a good deal of cogency that the really hard and meaningful governmental decisions respecting higher education are made in the executive branch, at the level on which programs are actually operated. It is certainly true that the host of seemingly small decisions made each day can in time add up to a basic approach or style of administration that can significantly change the original objectives of a program. Statutory provisions are generally broad enough to permit choices among alternative interpretations wide enough apart to determine the very direction of a program. To be specific, administrators of research programs face, with each new contract or grant, the choice between whether to deal with the strong, admittedly competent institution or to take a risk with the less strong but perhaps promising institutions. The accumulation of these decisions in an individual program and throughout the Government results in a basic approach to a key policy question.

No matter how competent the individual administrator, however, or how broad and farsighted the particular agency, there exists constantly in Government the need to see things large; to escape agency parochialism and bureaucratic self-interest in order to get "the big picture." This section deals with the constitutional body whose responsibility it is to see and act on the big picture and with the variety of bodies charged from time to time with capturing for policy makers that same picture.

The Congress and Higher Education

Alexander Hamilton, in defense of the Constitution and of strong Government generally, pointed out that, if men were angels, there would be no need for governments. It is safe to say that the Congress of the United States was not designed to be populated by or to govern angels. Nevertheless, few aspects of Federal policy can be understood without an appreciation of the way they are dealt with by the Congress. For the Congress clearly has a central role in shaping policy, is ultimately responsible for putting it into law when necessary, sets the financial limits within which policies are executed, and stands as the ever-present eminence in whose shadow every executive decision is made.

Although the percentage of Congressmen with college degrees is substantially higher than in the constituencies they represent, interest in the problems of higher education is an acquired taste for most Congressmen, and understanding and sympathy for the objectives of higher education are never even acquired by some. The few members of each Congress with experience in the field of higher education usually choose to specialize in a policy area nearer their own academic interests or one that is more desirable for other reasons. For example, Senator J. William Fulbright, President of the University of Arkansas before coming to the Senate, chose foreign policy as his special area, although in the Fulbright Act he made a major educational contribution. Senator Paul Douglas, a distinguished professor of economics, devotes his major attention to economic affairs.

The fact is that the experience of most Congressmen, both before and after being elected to the Congress, is in areas far removed from education. Overwhelmingly, they are lawyers or farmers or businessmen, whose connection with higher education has most probably been limited to that of a more or less interested alumnus. This is an important fact, although not so important as some would make it. Politicians, as a group, and Congressmen, in particular, are not notably antiintellectual or antieducation. Some are, to be sure, but probably a smaller proportion than in the whole society. Occasionally the shrillest Congressional voices are from those who do not understand or sympathize with the processes of education, particularly that part which is dedicated to the search for truth whatever the cost in pain and punctured biases. Their voices have at times given a cast to the whole Congressional voice that has raised deep resentment and suspicion among educators. More important in the long run than these few, however, are the many who are open to persuasion and receptive to education about education.

The question of Congressional attitudes about higher education is crucial to the resolution of future problems in the field. Equally important, however, is the capacity of the Congress to deal with educational matters, even assuming the will to do so. The capacity of the Congress can only be understood against the background of its own operations and organization.

If the executive branch of the Government has grown by patches, it is partly because the patches have been applied by a Congress whose organization is itself quiltlike. The basic work of the Congress is, of course, done in its standing committees. By virtue of the division-of-labor system under which the Congress operates, each standing committee is supposed to be the source of expert knowledge on matters within its scope, and its recommendations on legislation are more likely than not to be accepted by the chamber of which it is a part. Obviously, this does not mean that legislation, as it comes from a committee, is never changed during the course of debate. What is true, however, is that the committees determine whether and in what form legislation will reach the floor and that committee members have had a greater opportunity than others to become expert in the intricacies of the legislation, the justification for its support, and arguments for its defeat. These are all important sources of power and influence.

In 1946, the Congress undertook a complete reorganization of its committee structure. The LaFollette-Monroney Act of that year eliminated committees that no longer had substantial jurisdiction, combined others, and in general sharpened the jurisdictional focus of the remaining committees. The result was a reduction of the number of standing committees in the House of Representatives from 48 to 19 and in the Senate from 33 to 15. In the face of constant pressures for the establishment of new committees, these numbers held until 1958, when the House authorized a standing Committee on Science and Astronautics and the Senate established a comparable Committee on Aeronautics and Space Sciences.

It is important to note that the new jurisdictions were set in 1946, before the postwar involvement of the Government in higher education took shape. As a result, and as a result also of old customs and traditional pressures, the Congress has not yet come to grips with the greatly increased network of relationships that now characterizes government–higher-education affairs. A brief canvass of committee jurisdictions will demonstrate this graphically.

Until 1958, the programs of the National Science Foundation fell within the scope of the Interstate and Foreign Commerce Committees of both Houses. Now they are handled by the Space Committees of the respective Houses. The educational-exchange programs of the State Department and the International Cooperation Administration are the responsibility of the Foreign Affairs Committee of the House and the Foreign Relations Committee of the Senate. All business relating specifically to the Land-Grant Colleges is handled by the Agriculture Committees. The Armed Services Committees are responsible for the research and development programs of the Defense Department, while the Joint Committee on Atomic Energy deals with the programs of the Atomic Energy Commission. The Committees on Banking and Currency handle the College Housing Loan Program, while the Interstate and Foreign Commerce Committee of the House and the Labor and Public Welfare Committee of the Senate have the National Institutes of Health under their wing. Finally, there is the Committee on Education and Labor in the House and the Committee on Labor and Public Welfare in the Senate. These are the Committees which ostensibly have jurisdiction over education generally. Actually, until the passage of the National Defense Education Act of 1958, these Committees were virtually dormant in the field of higher education, while the major programs affecting higher education were judged by the other committees just listed. One of the encouraging signs of the last several years has been the assumption of increasing responsibility by these two Committees for matters within their jurisdiction.

But this canvass would not be complete without accounting for those most influential of all Congressional agencies, the Committees on Appropriations and the Rules Committee of the House of Representatives. To take the latter first, the Rules Committee in the House of Representatives is the channel through which virtually all legislation flows to the floor of the House. The Rules Committee sets the length at which a measure may be debated, the number and kinds of amendments that may be offered, and, generally, the "rules" of the debate. The full House has the power to revise or reject the terms set by the Committee, but it rarely exercises that power. It may also, under certain conditions, bypass the Committee altogether, but that too is rare.

It is sometimes said that the Rules Committee is the "traffic cop" of the House. Perhaps so, but it is well to remember that the traffic cop, too, is a full-fledged law officer. In any event, as the long-time Chairman of the Committee, Howard Smith of Virginia, once said, "My folks didn't elect me to be a traffic cop."

The Rules Committee can and does exercise considerable influence over proposed legislation. It was, for example, the Committee's failure in the closing days of the 86th Congress to clear for floor action a request to have the school-construction bill sent to Conference that finally sealed the doom of that bill. The action of the Committee in that instance was important in triggering a successful move at the start of the next Congress to add to its membership so as to make the Committee more responsive to the leadership of the House and to the new Administration. With respect to education, at least, the result was not a great improvement. The enlarged Committee promptly refused to send to the floor of the House for debate all three of the Administration's education bills—school aid, higher-education construction and scholarships, and revision of the NDEA.[24]

The power of the Rules Committee is highly specialized and is essentially negative. It can block and it can delay, but it has no power to originate and little to impel. In contrast, the appropriations process arches over the entire legislative and administrative structure, for it determines within statutory authorizations the level at which every program will operate.

Of the two Committees on Appropriations, that in the House of Representatives is acknowledged to be the more important and influential. There are many reasons for this, but one will suffice here: by a rather dubious bit of constitutional interpretation, the House has successfully asserted that the power given it in the Constitution to initiate all revenue bills extends to spending bills as well. Thus, the President's Budget is first acted on by the House each year and any subsequent bargaining proceeds from the level it sets.

The power of the Appropriations Committees, and particularly the House Committee, is truly impressive, for it extends far beyond a mere determination of the proper level of Federal expenditures— as crucial as that in itself would be—and includes power over the largest policy matters or the smallest administrative details. Although the rules of both Houses forbid substantive legislation from being included in appropriations matters, it is no exaggeration to say that the Appropriations Committees are constantly involved in substantive issues and that their presence there is rarely challenged. Indeed, it can hardly be otherwise, for the nature of the appropriations process puts Committee members into the closest contact with administrative officials and necessarily involves them in program, as distinct from purely fiscal, review.

The Appropriations Committees are divided into subcommittees, each of which is responsible for the budgets of one or more executive agencies. Thus, the jurisdiction of these subcommittees coincides only roughly with the jurisdiction of the subject-matter standing committees. For example, legislative authority for the Land-Grant College Acts is vested in a single legislative committee, but appropriations power is divided among several subcommittees.

This is not a distinction without a difference, for the effective power over appropriations rests at the subcommittee level. The recommendations of these bodies are seldom overridden by the full committees, and these in turn are even more rarely changed on the floor of either House. Since the subcommittee chairman is the acknowledged wielder of power within his group, it is often within his power to effect important changes in the level of Government activity. He is not, of course, an entirely free agent, but his voice, within his chamber, is a good deal more persuasive than one among equals.

A sympathetic or hostile subcommittee chairman can be the

difference between life and death for a program, and when the chairmen of the House and Senate subcommittees are in agreement, their power can be awesome. A graphic example of this is the experience over the past few years of the National Institutes of Health. Representative John Fogarty and Senator Lister Hill, Chairmen of the House and Senate Appropriations Sub-committees with jurisdiction over that agency, are both staunch advocates of a rapidly accelerated program of health research and training. In this they have found considerable support among other members of the Congress but an equal amount of opposition from leaders of the executive branch. The dispute has been over the rate of increase for research and training funds and has centered on the capacity of institutions of higher education and the medical field generally to absorb and use effectively greatly increased funds. The following table illustrates the resolution of this dispute to date.

NATIONAL INSTITUTES OF HEALTH APPROPRIATIONS
(IN MILLIONS)

Fiscal year	Budget request	Appropriation	Increase
1955	$ 71.1	$ 81.2	$ 10.1
1956	89.1	97.6	8.5
1957	126.5	184.4	57.9
1958	190.1	211.2	21.1
1959	211.2	307.7	96.5
1960	294.3	400	105.7

In approving the fiscal year 1960 appropriation for the Department of Health, Education, and Welfare, the President was careful to make clear that he did not approve of the Congressional increase of more than $100 million for health research and training. He announced that three new criteria were to be applied to applications for research funds. It now had to be determined of each project:

1. That it is of such high priority and great promise that its deferment would be likely to delay progress in medical discovery

2. That it will not result in the harmful diversion of manpower

and other resources needed for teaching and medical-care services

3. That it will not bring about the substitution of Federal for non-Federal sources of support for medical research and training.

The battle continued, however, in the following year when the Senate Appropriations Sub-committee appointed a group of consultants to study and make recommendations on the proper level of Federal support for research and training in the health fields. This group recommended that the level of Government support ought to rise immediately to better than $650 million a year, a recommendation which the Committee accepted and wrote immediately into the Senate version of the 1961 appropriation bill.

The following table shows the disposition of the fiscal year 1961 appropriation for the National Institutes of Health (in millions of dollars):

	Budget request	House action	Senate action	Senate increases	Final
Research and training activities..	$205.598	$235.189	$285.070	$ 48.881	$260.000
Total NIH appropriation	400.000	455.000	664.000	209.000	560.000

It should be mentioned that a separate but related controversy concerning higher education is hidden among these figures. Probably no single issue of Government policy has been chewed over more in recent years than that concerning the amount the Government should pay for overhead costs incurred on a federally sponsored research project. Each year for the past several, the Senate has voted funds to raise the level of overhead payments from the present 15 per cent of direct costs to 25 per cent. Each year the House refuses to accede to this increase in Conference, and each year the increase is dropped. In fiscal year 1961, $22,681,000 of the total Senate increases was for that purpose. As usual, it failed to survive. It is significant that this issue, so important to institutions of higher education, is resolved, legislatively, entirely within the appropriations process.

Indeed, the significant feature of the NIH appropriations case is that at no point in the process has the subject-matter committee of either House which is responsible for higher education or health research been involved. The legislative consideration has been entirely within the framework of appropriations, and in both Houses this has essentially meant reliance on the judgment of the respective subcommittee chairmen.[25] Thus, legislative decisions with important consequences for higher education—and it is important to note that the question here is not the wisdom of these decisions—have been made without reference to the bodies which in theory have expert knowledge of the affected area.

It is extremely unlikely that the present Congressional pattern of dealing with higher education will be changed radically in the near future. For one thing, jurisdictional lines, once drawn among the committees, assume a life and a justification of their own and tend to be jealously protected; for another, the present pattern is partly the result of the mission-oriented character of most Federal programs. After all, the Defense Department *will* continue research and development work, and the fact that colleges and universities are involved does not lessen the responsibility of the Armed Services committees over the defense establishment as a whole.[26]

Finally, the existing fragmentation of jurisdiction probably represents in part a desire by the Congress to avoid coming to grips with the difficult problems that are a part of any discussion of Federal aid to education, as such. It is unquestionably easier to pretend that assistance for college facilities is really a housing problem and not an education problem, for to do so allows everyone gracefully to ignore whatever problems of Church-State and race relations are involved in education. It may well be that disorganization is a modest price to pay for such a luxury.

On the other side, however, it should be noted that the recent public interest in education is making this Congressional posture more and more difficult to maintain. As times goes on, the claims of higher education are likely to be pressed with greater vigor, and the underlying issues will come more sharply into focus. The Congress is a remarkably adaptable institution, and such a change, if it comes, will no doubt be reflected in the way educational issues are dealt with. Perhaps the beginnings of this change have been seen already in the hearings, debate, and action on the National Defense Education Act, for these immediate post-Sputnik activities were the most comprehensive examination ever made by the Congress of higher education. Significantly, they were undertaken by the Education Committees of both Houses. This educational process continued in 1961 as both groups considered proposed changes to NDEA as well as proposals for an academic facilities-building program and a scholarship program.

Thus, while dramatic changes are rarely visible in Congressional behavior, there is constant movement, as there is in any organism which is responsive to its environment. To those interested in the future of Federal activities in higher education, the subtleties of Congressional behavior will be worth watching from now on.

Commissions, Committees, and Presidential Advisors

It is probably true that a large bureaucratic organization is prone to two conflicting drives. On the one hand, each unit in it strives to distinguish itself from others that seem most like it. Even were no meaner motives involved, the professional pride that is a part of the sense of a uniquely important mission would suffice to keep that drive alive. On the other hand, there is also a compelling drive to coordinate—to keep in harmony the purposes and means of units which are functionally similar.

Actually, both of these characteristics are essential to the successful operation of a bureaucracy. The former supplies the motive power that keeps alive an indispensable sense of purpose, while the latter prevents the organization from flying apart. Furthermore, overwhelming dominance of one or the other can lead to chaos or stultification. The tension bred by the two in competition is healthy to the life of the organization.

Thus far we have focused on the separateness of Government activities in higher education, and properly so, for that has been and is their dominant characteristic. It would be an incomplete picture, however, were we not to account for the efforts toward togetherness. Several major efforts have been made since the end of World War II to point the way toward a national policy in higher education. The absence of a definable national policy indicates that these efforts were not met with universal acclamation, but they are no less worth considering for that.

THE PRESIDENT'S COMMISSION ON HIGHER EDUCATION (1946)

In 1946, President Truman appointed a Commission on Higher Education under the direction of the late George F. Zook, who was then President of the American Council on Education. The mandate of the Commission was no less than a reexamination of "our system of higher education in terms of its objectives, methods and facilities," and further "an examination of the functions of higher education in our democracy and of the means by which they can best be performed."

In response to this direction the Commission produced a report of considerable length which did not, according to one commentator, receive "unanimous acceptance from the academic community, nor did the Truman administration see fit to sponsor legislation to put into effect more than a small fraction of the program envisaged by the commission." [27]

The proposals of the Zook Commission were broad, far-reaching, and weighted toward public higher education. As such, they had little chance of being translated into public policy, for, as a rough rule of thumb, the chances of success for any set of recommendations increase as the proposals become more precise.

The Commission considered briefly the question of the organization of Federal programs in higher education.[28] This section of the report is interesting chiefly for its recommendation of greater centralization of powers in an education agency that would have greater prestige and status than the U.S. Office of Education did. Perhaps unfortunately, the Commission did not see fit to choose among the various possible ways of achieving that end. It did, however, contribute to the intelligent consideration of the subject by pointing out that Federal control of education—the awesome, if misunderstood, specter that hovers over all discussions of a centralized education administration—is quite as likely to result from the opposite.

One of the major recommendations of the Commission was "that any basic research program of the Federal Government . . . be carried on as largely as possible in the universities of the country, and therefore administered at the Federal level either by or in close relationship with the Federal agency which has due regard for all the functions of the university, particularly its teaching and its training of research workers." [29] Three years later Congress established the National Science Foundation as an independent agency to administer programs of basic research in the sciences.

THE HOOVER COMMISSION (1947)

While the President's Commission on Higher Education was still in the course of its deliberations, Public Law 162 of the 80th Congress established the Commission on Organization of the Executive Branch of the Government and President Truman appointed former President Herbert Hoover to chair the Commission. The Hoover Commission had a broad mandate to inquire into and make recommendations on the organization of all Federal executive functions. Inevitably, therefore, it became concerned with Federal education activities.

The major proposal of the Hoover Commission regarding education was that certain educational activities be combined with Federal welfare activities in a new department which would have cabinet status.[30] This new department was to contain an Educational Service and a Social Security Service at the same organizational level and directly responsible to the Office of the Secretary.

It is difficult to know just what the Commission had in mind for this new Educational Service to do in the area of higher education, for the report says:

> Concerning higher education, nine departments and agencies are making grants or entering into contracts for research without coordination for these programs. For years the Government has made payments for agricultural research. More recently, the Government has been spending huge sums in grants to higher institutions for atomic and military research. These projects are concentrated in the natural and physical sciences. The grants have an important effect on the educational system.
>
> There are those who believe that these various educational programs should be concentrated in the Office of Education. This Commission believes, however, that these educational programs must be administered by the agencies whose functions the particular programs serve to promote.[31]

It is significant that the Commission evidently rejected the proposals of its advisory task force. This group recommended the establishment of a Federal Education Agency, preferably as an independent unit free of departmental affiliation; a National Board of Education; and a career Commissioner of Education, preferably appointed by and responsible to the Board. It also recommended that all Federal activities affecting higher education, except those of a critical emergency nature, be judged by their impact on a balanced educational system, and that the Federal Government should not "pursue a course of promoting unrelated educational specialities or special interests." [32] Finally, the Task Force recommended that the Federal Education Agency be responsible for the development of and advice on Federal policies in higher education and for coordination of all Federal activities in higher education. Until that could be achieved, it recommended the establishment, as a stop-gap measure, of an interagency coordinating committee.[33] The Hoover Commission itself accepted none of these proposals.

The Hoover Commission wobbled from the wild improbability of some of its Task Force's proposals to the bland ambiguity of the full Commission's recommendation. Its impact on Federal activities in higher education was not great.

THE PRESIDENT'S COMMITTEE ON EDUCATION BEYOND THE HIGH SCHOOL (1956)

The same cannot be said with complete accuracy of the Committee on Education Beyond the High School appointed by President Eisenhower in 1956. The years between 1948 and 1956 were not barren of commissions, committees, and reports, but 1956 was the next Federal attempt, after the two just discussed, to evaluate the whole of the Federal role in higher education. This Committee, headed by Devereaux C. Josephs, Chairman of the Board of the New York Life Insurance Company, showed a generally more conservative approach in assessing the Federal role than did the Zook Commission. As a result, its recommendations were on the whole less sweeping, and perhaps more attainable.

None of this, however, had much to do with its relative success, for unpredictable external events gave its report and recommendations a prominence they could not otherwise have hoped to achieve. Specifically, the Committee issued its second, and major, report in July, 1957. In October of that year the first Russian satellite went into orbit and American higher education became overnight a prime object of public, and hence political, concern. Efforts toward new Federal programs in higher education suddenly were skyrocketed to top legislative and executive priority, and the Josephs Committee report, which had stimulated some of these efforts, went right along with them.[34]

Again, as with the Zook Commission, the specific substantive recommendations of the Committee are of less concern here than were its efforts to bring order into the administrative and policy-making apparatus of the Federal Government. The Committee had one major proposal on this score. First, it said:

> In the light of the serious national and international problems that require the United States to be educated to its full capacity,

the occasional appointment of temporary committees is inadequate to deal with the needs for national leadership and coordinated Federal activity in the field of post–high school education. The Committee believes that in addition to those permanent and temporary committees now operating in connection with some of the Government programs relating to this field, permanent machinery should be created, with provision for broadly representative lay and professional advisors, to keep under continuous scrutiny all Federal programs affecting education beyond the high school and to advise the President and the heads of appropriate Federal agencies with respect thereto. . . .

The Committee, therefore, urgently recommends that the President authorize and direct the Secretary of Health, Education, and Welfare to develop for his consideration specific proposals on the best means for setting up whatever machinery may be necessary (*a*) to further a continuous and orderly review and development of the national and intergovernmental aspects of education beyond the high school and (*b*) to fulfill the other needs relating thereto which are identified in these conclusions and recommendations.[35]

With respect to the first part of the Committee's proposal, no such committee has yet been established. Indeed, for several years, the Secretary of Health, Education, and Welfare has had the statutory authority to appoint a National Advisory Committee on Education. The option has not been exercised, largely on the grounds that to do so would undercut the authority of the Commissioner of Education, who, after all, serves to advise the Secretary on educational matters.

The second part of the proposal has fared somewhat better, however, for while no Presidential Committee was forthcoming, the National Defense Education Act, some thirteen months later, did direct the Secretary of Health, Education, and Welfare to

advise and consult with the heads of departments and agencies of the Federal Government responsible for the administration of scholarship, fellowship, or other educational programs with a view to securing full information concerning all specialized scholarship, fellowship, or other educational programs administered by or under any such department or agency and to developing policies and procedures which will strengthen the educational programs and objectives of the institutions of higher education utilized for such purposes by any such department or agency.

This provision falls short of the more ambitious scheme envisaged by the Committee, but it represents, nevertheless, the highest sanction yet given to an internal governmental inquiry into ways of improving Federal practices in higher education. It is yet too early to judge the contribution which this study will make. All that can be said now is that the climate of opinion has never been more favorable for those who feel that the present arrangement is not all that might be desired.

Conclusion

Governmental advisory committees in the field of education start out with so many disadvantages that the true wonder is that they are able to accomplish anything at all. The first problem is that of who is to be represented on the committee, and the committee can easily founder on that reef before the first meeting is held. There must be, on every group, representatives of public and private institutions, and the group must be balanced geographically and represent major religious and economic interests. The result is often a group that cannot reach agreement on any but the broadest principles of virtue, generally, and good education in particular.[36]

Even the best advisory groups face two other important problems. First, the questions these groups are called on to resolve are complex and important or there would be no need for the group in the first place. Under the best of conditions, however, advisory groups meet only infrequently and must rely heavily on their staffs to provide information and even to frame alternatives. Indeed, the more "blue-ribbon" the committee is, the less time and attention it is likely to be able to devote to its task.[37]

Even beyond this set of difficulties, however, there is the fact that advisory committees are by definition impermanent beings without any self-sustaining powers that would provide the continuity and follow-through needed to translate advice into policy. Their recommendations are, after all, only that; to be accepted or rejected, pushed vigorously, mildly, or not at all, as the responsible officials see fit. All in all, advisory bodies face a formidable set of obstacles.

The three Commissions discussed here are the three that in the postwar period have been charged with the responsibility of examining the entire Federal effort in higher education. In addition, there have been a variety of other bodies which have scrutinized and made recommendations on particular parts of that effort. It would not be fair to say that these Commissions had no impact on Federal activities, but it is reasonable to be skeptical about the size of their contribution. There is a point, after all, at which recognition of problems and calls to meet them on the part of bodies with no responsibility for meeting them cease to be fruitful. There is, of course, value in having groups of able and respected people turn their attention to important national problems. But temporary committees which recommend the establishment of permanent committees lose a large share of their claim to public attention.

There is no reason to doubt the sincerity of the concern on the part of the Government over the disarray of the present Federal effort in higher education, or the genuine desire for a coherent set of policies that has led to the establishment of these Committees. There is reason to doubt, however, that Presidential Committees are the best means of turning that concern into effective policy. One such Committee wrote:

> The Federal Government has no inclusive and consistent public policy as to what it should or should not do in the field of education. Whatever particular policies it seems to be pursu-

ing are often inconsistent with each other, sometimes in conflict. They suggest a haphazard development, wherein policies of far-reaching effect have been set up as mere incidents of some special attempt to induce an immediate and particular efficiency.

Without a comprehensive, forward looking, and coherent public policy in regard to education, the present educational situation in the Federal Government cannot be greatly improved.

This was the judgment of the National Advisory Committee on Education, and it made its report to President Herbert Hoover in 1931.

NOTES

[1] Of at least equal importance, although not directly relevant to higher education, was the usefulness of the GI Bill in keeping the labor market from being inundated by returning veterans and in providing that when they did enter the labor force it would be with greater skills and better education than would otherwise have been possible.

[2] In 1961, the 87th Congress took an important step in the recognition of foreign aid as a long-term obligation. In that year development loans, the chief mechanism for economic assistance, were authorized for a five-year period. The Congress was unwilling, however, to relinquish its power of annual appropriation, so funds must still be appropriated each year even though the Executive is empowered to enter into multiyear agreements involving at least a moral commitment of loan funds. Thus, the Congress stepped forward with one foot but was not quite willing to bring the other alongside.

[3] Any discussion of Federal activities in the area of research support must start from the excellent work done by Charles V. Kidd, particularly in the book *American Universities and Federal Research* (Belknap Press, Harvard, 1959). The authors owe an obvious debt to Dr. Kidd for much of the data and some of the insights that have informed the analysis in this section.

[4] These percentages are derived from the data given in the National Science Foundation's *Reviews of Data on Research and Development,* April, 1960. Using base figures for 1953 to 1954, Kidd reports that 24 per cent was spent in the life sciences, 33 per cent in the physical sciences, 37 per cent in engineering, and 6 per cent in all other fields.

The proportion of funds going to social science research may increase in the years ahead because of two developments. The National Science Foundation announced in 1961 the establishment of a separate division concerned with the social sciences. The Foundation's definition of what constitutes "social science" for its purposes is a good deal more restrictive than most universities would accept for theirs. Second, the Cooperative Research Program of the Office of Education is growing. While it is a small program compared with others—not more than $5 million in fiscal year 1962—it has grown steadily since its start in 1954, and probably has not yet reached its full growth. Neither of these developments, however, will significantly alter the general picture.

[5] Charles V. Kidd, "New Government-University Relationships in Research," *Higher Education* (April, 1960), p. 3.

[6] One official of a major Eastern university says that Government and universities share the same goals but put them in a different order of priority: The Government sets research first and teaching second, while universities are primarily teaching institutions and research producers secondarily. This view is charitable to both parties.

[7] We do not suggest that it is the job of Government agencies to decide what colleges and universities "as a whole" ought to be doing. We do suggest that these agencies have a considerable impact on what institutions will do, and that their powers ought to be exercised with due regard for the larger educational context in which institutions operate. What *institutions* ought to do in response to the availability of large sums of money for a fairly narrow part of their total operation is another question, which is quite as important as the one with which we have dealt.

Furthermore, we should point out that the NIH research funds have been absorbed by institutions and that the demand has always outstripped the supply—even at the increased levels. The question, as we shall show in more detail later, is always of priorities and the possible distorting effects of making large sums of money available for objects that may be lower in priority within institutions than others for which money is not available.

[8] An admirably candid statement on this point was made to the Intergovernmental Relations Sub-committee of the House Committee on Government Operations in August, 1961, by Dr. James A. Shannon, Director of the National Institutes of Health: "Although these grants will, in certain cases, serve developmental purposes, they are primarily

designed to give institutions with active research programs the means for exercising greater freedom and initiative in developing new approaches. . . .

"If [under regular NIH research support programs] . . . an institution has not been able to get approval for a single grant, it must be assumed that its research work has been of a fairly low standard. If this is the case, it is probably true that its teaching program, its faculty, and its facilities also need strengthening. In that case, the problem is one of general educational support. It is my personal opinion that this is, in fact, a serious national problem on which action is already long overdue but it is not a problem for which NIH has either the authority or the means to address itself."

[9] This panel, chaired by Chancellor Glenn T. Seaborg of the University of California at Berkeley, reported to the President late in 1960. It is too early to know what, if any, effect its recommendation will have on the actual operation of research programs, but a mechanism—the President's Science Advisor—does exist through which they may be pressed, if the will to do so exists.

Among its more specific recommendations, the Seaborg Panel proposed:

a. Federal support for basic research and graduate education in the sciences should be continued and flexibly increased so as to support excellence where it already exists and to encourage new centers of outstanding work.

b. Long-term Federal research support for broad objectives.

c. The Federal Government should seek forms of support that would permit universities to enlarge their permanent facilities.

d. Federal support for facilities and equipment for research and graduate education.

e. Wherever feasible, new research undertakings should be established in, or in close association with, universities, and existing government installations should develop closer relations with graduate education and university scientists.

f. General Federal policy governing basic research and graduate education should be formulated under the leadership of the Office of the President.

On the last item, the Committee said further, ". . . it is self-evident that the government should have the means for a well-coordinated and powerfully directed general policy." We can only add that the need may be self-evident, but the desire to meet the need is far from universal.

[10] Kidd, *American Universities and Federal Research,* p. 5.

[11] The 1961 Act for International Development—the foreign-aid act—abolished the International Cooperation Administration and created in its place the Agency for International Development (AID). We shall continue to use the old name of the agency when referring to activities for which it was responsible.

[12] There are signs that better days may be ahead in this respect. First, the former position of Special Assistant to the Secretary of State for Educational and Cultural Affairs was upgraded in 1961 to a full Assistant Secretaryship—a welcome recognition of the importance of this activity. Second, the Department of Health, Education, and Welfare asked the Congress in 1961 for an Assistant Secretary to coordinate its international activities and to give it representation within Government circles at the policy-making level. And third, in the First Session of the 87th Congress, the Senate and House passed a bill sponsored by Senator Fulbright which would give the President authority to assign responsibility for virtually every existing major international education program to whatever agency he saw fit. Thus, the conditions may soon be present for a genuine ordering of the Government's house in this important field.

[13] In addition to its direct fellowship program, the National Institutes of Health support a large number of graduate students, and some undergraduates, in its training grants programs. Not even NIH knows how many students are supported in these programs, for each university department receiving a grant for a training program has considerable discretion in deciding how many students it will assist. It is a reflection of the lack of pattern in the Federal effort that not even the administrators of these large programs have accurate data on this important aspect of them.

[14] A notable exception to this generalization was the virtual withdrawal of the Atomic Energy Commission from the fellowship field following the establishment of broader scientific support by the National Science Foundation. The AEC, however, continues to operate small fellowship programs, in health physics, industrial hygiene, industrial medicine, and nuclear science and engineering.

[15] At a later point, we shall discuss at some length the deficiencies of the academic community in dealing with the Government. Therefore,

we shall only note here the absence of visible concern or activity on the part of academic people on this issue of great importance to them. Perhaps this was accounted for in part by the fact that the actions discussed above occurred in the summer of 1961. The Congress is in session in the summer even if colleges and universities are not.

[16] The Foundation itself showed its concern over this concentration of its fellows by instituting the so-called Cooperative Graduate Program which spread awards over a much larger number of universities. Under this program in 1959, 14.6 per cent of the students in physics were enrolled at the institutions listed above and 67 schools in all had Cooperative fellows in physics.

[17] In 1961, the Kennedy Administration proposed that the fellowship program be enlarged and that a sizable number of awards be given in an open competition, with the winners free to attend the school of their choice. This arrangement would clearly benefit some institutions, but representatives of organized higher education almost unanimously urged the Congress to require that all fellowships be allotted to institutions and that they not be allowed to pile up at only a few. In this case, the many spoke with louder voices than the few.

[18] The Administration in 1961 proposed a program of institutes for teachers of English. The House Committee, after a good deal of discussion of the danger of the Government's sponsoring the study of literature (grammar and spelling seem to be acceptable), voted to limit the institutes to the study of English as a foreign language. The Senate Committee, on the other hand, not only accepted the English proposal, but voted to add institutes for training secondary school teachers in subjects related to foreign affairs. Clearly, the Congress is groping for an acceptable Federal role in this area.

[19] The ROTC and their effect on institutions have only recently been the object of serious study by people other than those immediately involved. See particularly Gene M. Lyons and John W. Masland, *Education and Military Leadership*, 1959.

[20] Raymond F. Howes, Staff Associate of the American Council on Education, put it this way in a speech to a group of college business officers in 1956: "A program of Federal aid . . . has the following characteristics: (1) The motive is to assist institutions to achieve objectives which they themselves have established. (2) An actual Federal subsidy for such activities is involved. (3) The subsidy is administered in such a way as to give the largest measure of assistance to the institutions in greatest financial need.

"It is a strange fact that although the Federal Government spends well over a billion dollars a year on programs which directly or indirectly increase the income of colleges and universities, one can search diligently and still not find a program that meets all these elements in the definition of Federal aid."

[21] *Proceedings of the 72nd Annual Convention of the American Association of Land-Grant Colleges and State Universities.* (Washington, D.C., 1958), pp. 302–303.

[22] For some educators the question here has been the always intriguing one of whether to press for long-range goals at a possible risk to short-run advantages. This group—probably not large, but significant nevertheless—would have preferred to see the College Housing Loan Program administered by the Office of Education, but they have been reluctant to press the point for fear of embroiling the program in controversy, both administrative and Congressional.

[23] The Kennedy Administration proposed to the 87th Congress a program of loans for the construction of academic facilities. The proposal met with virtually unanimous opposition from the higher-education community, and was quickly changed by the House Education and Labor Committee to a program which would combine matching grants and loans. The Administration readily accepted the change. This bill was one of the three stymied by the House Rules Committee in the First Session of the 87th Congress.

[24] It is arguable whether the Rules Committee can or does act in such a way as to frustrate the wishes of a determined majority in the House. Often its failure to act on a controversial piece of legislation may be a reflection of the unwillingness of a controlling number of House members to press the issue strongly and the wish of others to be spared the embarrassment of voting on the issue. It is likely that the infrequency with which the Committee is overruled or bypassed is testimony not only to the difficulty of those procedures, but to the political sensitivity of the Committee members, as well.

[25] The power structure of the Senate is such that senior members of substantive Committees, particularly Chairmen or ranking minority members, are often members of the Appropriations Committee, and because of their seniority may be Sub-committee Chairmen on that Committee. For example, Senator Lister Hill, Chairman of the Labor and Public Welfare Committee, is also head of the Appropriations Subcommittee that deals with HEW. This system of interlocking power within the Senate provides a measure of continuity between substantive

and appropriations policy that is almost wholly lacking in the House where members are limited to one major Committee.

[26] A partial exception to this generalization may emerge in the area of international education, where the Education Committees in both Houses have been showing a more vigorous interest, beginning in about 1958 with the enactment of the Language Development Program in NDEA. With their appetites thus whetted, the Committees have begun to look more carefully at other international aspects of education.

[27] Richard G. Axt, *The Federal Government and Financing Higher Education* (New York, 1952), p. 190.

[28] *Higher Education for American Democracy* (Washington, D.C., 1947), Vol. III, pp. 35–50.

[29] *Ibid.,* p. 47.

[30] The proposals are contained in Report No. 17, on Social Security and Education. Three dissenting Commissioners argued for the inclusion of the health function in the new department, and the general principle which they supported carried the day, ultimately, in the establishment of the Department of Health, Education, and Welfare.

[31] *Ibid.,* pp. 31–32.

[32] *Functions and Activities of the National Government in the Field of Welfare,* prepared for the Commission on Organization of the Executive Branch of the Government (Washington, D.C., 1949), p. 365.

[33] The Zook Commission proposed coordination by the Office of Education, and until that could be worked out, it also proposed an interagency committee, chaired by the Commissioner of Education, to consult with and advise agencies operating educational programs.

[34] Even before the dramatic events of that autumn, plans were being made to translate the major recommendations of the Committee into a legislative program. Marion B. Folsom, then Secretary of Health, Education, and Welfare, had appointed a group within the Department to perform that task. Thus, the Department was not completely off balance when this job suddenly became number one on the priority list.

[35] The President's Committee on Education Beyond the High School, *Second Report to the President* (Washington, D.C., 1957), p. 25.

[36] It is instructive to contrast this general Federal practice with the recent Committee on Higher Education in the State of New York. This was a group composed of three members, Marion B. Folsom of Eastman Kodak and a former U.S. Secretary of Health, Education, and Welfare, John W. Gardner of the Carnegie Corporation, and Henry Heald of the Ford Foundation. This group, which made no attempt to

be representative of all interests in New York higher education, made a report of far greater specificity than any comparable national group. The effect of this Committee's recommendations on higher education in New York State has been impressive.

[37] There is a corollary issue which should not be overstressed but should be mentioned. It is the question of where the staff for a commission should be drawn from. If composed of agency people on temporary assignment, there can be a real problem in neutralizing institutional loyalties and broadening perspectives. If taken from outside the Government, the problem of educating the staff can be quite as great as that of educating the members.

The difficulties are not insurmountable, but they do add to the handicaps temporary committees must overcome.

CHAPTER THREE

THE POSTURE OF HIGHER EDUCATION

THE ORGANIZATION OF ORGANIZATIONS

If the organization of Government to deal with higher education seems unduly complex and confusing, it may put things in perspective to look at the other side of the coin: higher education's organization to deal with the Federal Government. Complex structure and bureaucratic characteristics are not the exclusive properties of the Government.

Probably no other segment of American society has so many organizations and is yet so unorganized as higher education. The U.S. Office of Education lists more than a hundred "national organizations" in the field of higher education, many of which are proliferated in regional and State subparts. It is a rare college or university that does not belong to more than one of these organizations, and a rare staff member who does not maintain individual membership in at least one. So varied, overlapping, and uneven in size are these organizations that they defy generalization. At best, it can be said that they fairly reflect the pluralism of American higher education. For the purpose of this discussion it will serve to report that more than a score of such national organizations maintain offices and staffs of varying size in Washington, D.C., from which fact it may be presumed that at least these organizations take an active interest in relationships with the Federal Government. In their lack of uniformity this group of organizations has all the characteristics of an accurate sample of the total. Some have memberships consisting of institutions of higher education, while others have individual memberships. Associations of institutions may represent types of institutions, others institutions of a particular size or type of control. There are, for example, the Association of American Colleges, the American Association of Colleges for Teacher Education, the American Association of Junior Colleges, and the Council for the Advancement of Small Colleges, Inc. Among the associations that represent institutions on the basis of their type of control or source of support are the National Catholic Education Association, the Council of Protestant Colleges and Universities, and the State Universities Association. Lest this appear altogether too simple and obvious, it should be pointed out that the State Universities Association consists only of those State universities that are not designated as land-grant institutions; State universities that are land-grant institutions are members of the American Association of Land-Grant Colleges and State Universities. To tidy things up, there exists an organization known as the National Association of State Universities, which happily includes in its membership all comprehensive State universities, whether they be land-grant or not. The tidiness of this arrangement was disrupted in 1961 by the creation of a fourth organization, known as the Association of State Colleges and Universities, consisting principally of institutions formerly regarded as teachers colleges but recently broadened in scope and designated as State colleges and universities. Just how the complexities of this situation will be unraveled is by no means clear.

Of the associations having individual membership, most limit their membership and representation to persons holding specific positions in colleges and universities or having specialized areas of interest. Perhaps the best known of these is the American Association of University Professors. Persons involved in alumni affairs are organized in the American Alumni Council, while publicists and development officers are represented by the American College Public Relations Association (which in 1960 came close to renaming itself "The Association for the Advancement of Understanding and Support of Higher Education"). There is a recently arrived Washington representative of the National Association of College and University Business Officers, and it is expected there will soon be one for the deans of the Nation's graduate schools. Only the Association for Higher Education (a division of the National Education Association) among the organizations having individual memberships welcomes to its fold all persons engaged in the practice of higher education.

Several professional organizations largely oriented to higher education—such as the American Historical Association—though represented in Washington, appear to be located in the Nation's capital more for reasons of geographic convenience than out of any concern for relationships with the Federal Government. Notable exceptions are those professional organizations in the sciences, such as the American Association for the Advancement of Science and the National Academy of Sciences, whose extensive involvement in Federal programs gives them a vital interest in the affairs of Government.

A few significant and interested national organizations in higher education are notably not represented by staff in Washington. The American Association of Universities, for example, limits its representation to legal counsel engaged to deal with specific problems or issues, such as the oath and disclaimer provisions of the 1958 National Defense Education Act. But it is accurate to say that virtually every college and university in the United States has some degree of representation in Washington and access to one or more staffs in Washington.

While their memberships are large, the Washington staff of these organizations is usually small. With a few exceptions, national

organizations in higher education are represented in Washington by an Executive Secretary, who may have an assistant in addition to a small secretarial and clerical staff. So small are the staffs that the majority of them can be and are housed in a single building at 1785 Massachusetts Avenue, a building owned by the American Council on Education. Indeed, so many educational organizations are housed in that one building that the amusement was widespread some years ago when an official located in the building received a telegram addressed to the "American Carnival on Education."

The American Council on Education

Overarching the myriad associations of types of institutions and interested individuals in higher education is one supereducational association, the American Council on Education. Though it now encompasses a good many other activities, the American Council on Education is in a very real sense a creature of the relationship between the Federal Government and higher education. It was brought into being in 1918 in an effort to "coordinate the services which educational institutions and organizations could contribute to the Government in the national crisis brought on by World War I." Its membership was originally limited to a handful of other educational associations,[1] each of which had its particular interests and concerns, but which sought to establish a forum for cooperative and combined effort. The American Council on Education now reflects within its total membership of 1,222 all the complexities and diversities that characterize American education as such. Essentially, the membership consists of 82 *constituent* members (national and regional educational associations), 63 *associate* members which are national organizations in fields related to education, and 1,076 *institutional* members. Over the years, the Council has broadened the scope of its interests far beyond the coordination of services to the Federal Government. It now conducts surveys and studies, does research, and has an extensive program of publications, all of which are designed to promote the cause of higher education outside the context of Federal activities.[2]

The American Council on Education operates basically through a committee structure. For the purposes of this volume, the Council's Committee on Relationship of Higher Education to the Federal Government is the key committee.[3] Given the vast and varied nature of the American Council on Education's membership, it is not surprising to find that the Council's Committee principally concerned with Federal Government activities is itself broadly representative of American higher education. It is also not surprising to find that the membership on this Committee reflects varying views on current legislative issues and that it is sometimes unable to achieve a positive consensus on these issues. Occasionally the Committee turns to the membership of the Council proper and actually polls the membership to ascertain their sympathies or inclinations on current issues. It is an interesting commentary that the members of this Committee, who in the course of their service on the Committee achieve a fairly high degree of political awareness and understanding, should turn even infrequently to the Council's membership at large (which can be assumed to be relatively unfamiliar and unsophisticated in such matters) to get its direction on key legislative issues. It is at least an indication of their great concern lest they run too far ahead of general consensus among educators.[4]

In practice, the Committee on Relationships (as it is known in shorthand) consists of some 16 members and meets on the average of three times a year. The Committee is supported by professional staff members of the American Council on Education and by the Executive Secretaries of major national educational organizations located in Washington, who serve as consultants to the Committee. Additionally, the Committee on Relationships frequently invites as observers to its meetings representatives of Federal agencies operating programs in the area of higher education, and even legislators who have an interest in or a position on matters falling within the Committee's purview. Thus, the Committee has access in its deliberation to well-informed persons.

The usual practice of the Committee is to meet in "open session" for half a day, during which consultants and outside observers take part in a discussion of current issues. The Committee then goes into an afternoon executive session, at which time it attempts to hammer out legislative and other governmental policies for the American Council. Until recently, the net product of a given Committee session was likely to be simply a list of formal actions or resolutions of the Committee, without amplification or explanation. Late in 1960, the Committee on Relationships inaugurated the practice of referring tentative decisions to its constituent members for consideration and comment. While this has certain obvious advantages within the "politics" of higher education, it also has the very great advantage of involving a wider group of leaders in the decision-making process, outside the unsatisfactory atmosphere of the annual convention. Whether or not it will have the added effect of bringing more educators up to the level of political sophistication of the Committee itself remains to be seen.

Nonetheless, the format of this referral to major constituent agencies is exceedingly interesting, especially as it reflects an outgrowth of the experience described later in this chapter as a "case study." On December 10, 1960, the Executive Secretaries and elected heads of a dozen major national organizations [5] were convened for what was called a "Seminar on Federal Relationships." A background memorandum raised the basic questions, "Is higher education properly organized to get *all* it should?" and "Is higher education properly organized to get the *kind* of assistance it *wants?*" The answer was negative, at least in tone:

> There are undeniable weaknesses in the present system. The Council's Committee on Relationships of Higher Education to the Federal Government, while quite competent through knowledge and experience to devise policies in the best interest

of higher education, can bring little pressure to bear on constituent organizations, which sometimes take positions on Federal legislation after general discussion at annual meetings without the benefit of the detailed staff work essential to fully informed judgments. On numerous occasions the show of near-unity by representatives of national organizations in Congressional committee hearings has been achieved by presenting testimony in such a way as to minimize differences clearly on the record. This much can be achieved by agreement among the executive secretaries; but frequently it is not enough. There is need for closer year-round liaison among the major educational organizations on Federal legislative issues.

It is evident from this, and from the structure and process of the Committee on Relationships, that its usefulness is limited to setting fairly broad guidelines for policy. It is a strategic rather than a tactical instrument, and the practice of referring recommendations to the membership at large, while useful for other organizational purposes, limits further its flexibility as a policy-making body.[6] That considerations of this nature are important in determining an organization's effectiveness will become clearer in the legislative case study which will be discussed later in this chapter.

Finally, the Committee on Relationships, like the American Council on Education itself, is a representative body. As such it represents all the disagreements of American higher education as well as its agreements. In contrast to the educational associations that represent relatively homogeneous constituencies, the Committee and the American Council may suffer from the need to be virtually all things to all interests in the area of American higher education. Council leaders, whose long awareness of this problem has been sharpened by the abrasion of growing Federal programs, undertook in 1961 an initial review of the Council's activities, membership, and organization. Foundation-financed review by outside consultants may well result in a leaner membership list, tighter organization, and more assertive Council policies.

Activities

Recognizing that it is exceedingly dangerous to generalize about Washington representation, there is nonetheless a general pattern of activities common to them all. First of all, these headquarters plan and manage the many meetings and inevitable annual conventions of their several organizations. They frequently arrange appointments in Washington for members of their organizations and carry out a miscellaneous assortment of missions and/or errands for member organizations or individuals. Most of them prepare and disseminate to their membership reports of, among other things, legislative and administrative activities of the Federal Government affecting their constituencies. The American Council on Education bulletin, *Higher Education and National Affairs,* is the most widely circulated. Notable also is the occasional newsletter of the American Association of Land-Grant Colleges and State Universities, prepared by its Executive Secretary and former journalist, Russell P. Thackrey. Its circulation is strictly limited to the presidents of land-grant institutions, partly at least because this makes it possible for the editor to report more candidly than he might if addressing a wider audience.

One of the principal activities of the Executive Secretaries located in Washington is to "monitor" established operating Federal programs. They are sensitive to criticisms of operating policies and decisions, which they hear from their membership in the field, and they are effective in relaying these criticisms to responsible officials of the executive branch of government. The Executive Secretaries meet informally and frequently with key officials throughout the executive branch and have established over the years an admirable working relationship with these officials.

The Washington representatives of higher-education associations are frequently asked to serve on advisory committees to a variety of Federal agencies, such as the Advisory Committee on the College Housing Loan Program. In these capacities, they generally take a position or point of view established by the Association they represent, but it is not an uncommon practice for them to offer personal evaluations and judgments helpful to Government administrators. Most of the Executive Secretariat, and all of that part which represents institutional memberships, meets more or less regularly with the Commissioner of Education. The basic purpose of these monthly meetings is to keep the Executive Secretaries and their memberships abreast of Office of Education activities and policy developments and, secondarily, to give the Office of Education an opportunity to hear directly both comment and complaint from the Associations and their representatives.

The monitoring function of national organizations located in Washington is generally regarded by all concerned to be of exceedingly great value both to higher education and to the Government. It is a delicate function to perform, nonetheless. In the ideal, Executive Secretaries offer advice without attempting to administer, and cooperate without becoming captive to, the programs of the several agencies. The relationship calls for integrity on the part of both Government and nongovernment personnel. Though the distinction between Government and nongovernment is sometimes made indistinct as a result of personal cooperation, each must be aware always that the line does exist.

The reason for keeping the line visible between Government and nongovernment is particularly compelling in the field of education. It is all too easy for both parties to act on the facile assumption that education is after all a good thing, and that there is, therefore, a natural harmony of interests among all those working in the field. To an impressive degree this is true, but we have already seen instances in which the interest of the Government in obtaining particular service from higher education may come in conflict with the objectives of educational institutions. The job of "monitoring" the Government is an important one, as is the task of interpreting education to the Government, and vice versa. None of these jobs is so important, however, as to risk the independence and the freedom to pursue the individual interests of each party.

In a few instances, this distinction between the public role of Government and the independent role of national associations has been breached with no apparent ill effects. The National Academy of Sciences,[7] for example, virtually administers the graduate fellowship programs of the National Science Foundation; the American Council on Education manages the Department of State's program of American schools in Latin America and performs services for other Federal agencies under contract. Without raising any question with regard to the integrity of these relationships, it is possible to question how far such sharing of governmental responsibilities can be developed without rendering difficult a relationship that has been built on a concept of mutual independence and separation of functions.

Legislative Activities

All the organizations and their Executive Secretaries take an interest in legislative affairs, though this interest and the extent to which it is actively expressed vary enormously among them. One distinguished representative of higher education in Washington, who has served almost a decade in his post, boasts that he has never once, since he assumed his present position, set foot in the halls of Congress. Other association representatives are in close and fairly constant touch with at least key members of educational committees of the House and Senate. But even in these cases it requires some stretching of the definition to say that they "lobby" for higher education. The associations, through their Executive Secretaries, do seek invitations to testify on legislative matters of interest to them. A common practice is for a distinguished educator from among the association's membership to come to Washington and present a statement (ordinarily prepared by the Washington staff) to the appropriate committee, reflecting the views of the organization.

National organizations in higher education take positions on legislative matters only where there has been, in effect, express agreement among the membership. This can be, and has on some occasions proved to be, a cumbersome practice. Taking, for example, the 1960 discussion of possible legislation to provide assistance in the construction of academic facilities in higher education, it is fair to say that many associations that might have been spokesmen for the educational interests of the Nation had simply not adopted positions on the issue, or had adopted sufficiently inflexible positions, so that it was impossible for their representatives in Washington to work effectively for the legislation.

A Case Study

The illustration is worth pursuing. In 1960, the College Housing Loan Program was rounding out a decade of activity, but the question of its receiving additional lending authority was in doubt. Loans under the Program, made at interest rates based on the rate paid by the Federal Government on all its national debt obligations (plus ½ of 1 per cent for administration), had been available in 1959 to colleges and universities at 3⅛ per cent. The incumbent Republican Administration objected to this attractive rate of interest on the grounds that it was less than the Treasury of the United States itself had to pay for loans of similar maturity. The Administration proposed, as an alternative to the College Housing Loan Program, an ingenious but complicated program of "debt-retirement assistance." Under it, direct cash grants to the institution would be made in amounts and in such a way as to assist institutions that borrowed on the private money market to get a "net effective interest rate" approximately equal to that of the College Housing Loan Program. An energetic debate followed. The existing College Housing Loan Program was perhaps the only program on which all higher-education associations were agreed in their support. The Program had made more than a billion dollars in loans available to colleges and universities throughout the United States and in recent years had come to account for $1 of every $4 spent for construction in higher education throughout the country. In a rare demonstration of unanimity and action, higher-education associations first urged the Administration to remand its proposal, and then urged the Congress to disregard it. Secretary of Health, Education, and Welfare Arthur S. Flemming, acknowledging the views of higher education but aware at the same time of the firmness of Administration fiscal positions, worked hard through the Second Session of the 86th Congress to achieve some kind of compromise.

Meantime, legislation to extend the lending authority of the College Housing Loan Program was running into trouble in the Congress. Historically a part of the "omnibus" housing bill, the college loan program was suffering from the unpopularity of some of its housing bedfellows. The Senate version of the "omnibus" bill included funds for public housing, to which many Southerners, particularly in the House of Representatives, objected on the grounds that it could lead to Federal enforcement of residential desegregation. Secretary Flemming on a number of occasions warned the educational associations that their pet College Housing Loan Program was in jeopardy and suggested enactment of the debt-retirement-assistance alternative, so that "something would be on the books" in the event the College Housing Loan Program failed of passage. This was but one of the many compromise solutions suggested at one time or another during the Second Session of the 86th Congress. Another was a possible "omnibus" educational bill that would include additional funds for the College Housing Loan Program and Federal funds for academic facilities, the latter to be provided both through the Administration's grant device and through a program of direct, lump-sum, matching grants for the construction of non-revenue-producing facilities.

The possibility of the latter approach came as something of a surprise to representatives of higher education. Though lump-sum grants along the lines of the Hill-Burton Hospital Construction Program had been endorsed by the President's Committee on Education Beyond the High School in 1957, no responsible agency or organization had seen fit to recommend such a program. Much fear was expressed, if only privately, that such grants would raise the "Church-State issue" and open up a controversy from which higher education might suffer seriously.[8] Indeed, this objection had been raised to the Administration's proposal, since it embodied the principle of direct grants to institutions of higher education, both public and private. The College Housing Loan Program had avoided these issues, of course, because it was a loan program. Administration spokesmen argued that substantial benefits accrued to institutions, both public and private, under the College Housing Loan Program, as evidenced by its popularity; they took the position that, while this assistance to church-related institutions (among others) was not particularly obvious, it was nonetheless real. Thus, they argued that no new "principle" would be established by direct grants.

A number of members of Congress, notably Senator Joseph S. Clark of Pennsylvania, appeared to be confused by the lack of clarity of higher education's position, beyond their established unanimous support of college housing. When the subject of Federal assistance for nonhousing facilities came up, "American higher education" simply had no position. To be sure, the President's Committee on Education Beyond the High School had recommended such assistance, in the form of lump-sum matching grants. The Administration had recommended debt-retirement assistance to be applied to such facilities. Senator Clark himself had introduced a bill that would have provided direct Federal loans, on the same terms as the housing loans, for academic facilities. Here were three clear-cut possibilities to assist the Nation's colleges and universities in building the classrooms, laboratories, libraries, and other academic facilities they said they needed so badly. And the "omnibus" bill would have offered all three.[9]

A number of witnesses before the Senate subcommittee on which Senator Clark sat had hinted their personal support of direct matching grants as opposed to loans, largely on the grounds that borrowing for construction purposes, while sound in the case of revenue-producing facilities such as dormitories, would be essentially unsound if applied to non-revenue-producing facilities such as classrooms. They feared, they said, that the costs of construction financed in this way would have to be passed on to already hard-pressed students. Several higher-education associations had in fact debated the possibility of direct matching grants for academic facilities. The American Association of Land-Grant Colleges and State Universities, at its annual meeting in St. Louis in November, 1959, had argued the issue for many hours. It was clear that a majority of the member institutions favored such Federal assistance for the construction of academic facilities on land-grant campuses, but a number of members balked at the idea of making such direct assistance available to private and especially church-related institutions. The final resolution adopted by the Land-Grant Association endorsed such assistance for its own member institutions, but did not "presume" to recommend a form of assistance for those institutions not members of its Association! The Association of American Colleges, an organization made up of largely private institutions, including many with religious affiliations, had met in Boston in January, 1960, and considered a resolution from its Legislative Committee, authorizing that Committee to support "the most suitable form" of Federal aid to assist the Nation's colleges in meeting their physical-facilities needs. The resolution was adopted, but only after assurances had been demanded and given that "the Association would not be committed, without further reference to the membership, to any proposal involving outright grants." The membership did not feel it could endorse such an "open-end" authorization, because it was unable to resolve itself on the question of "the separation of Church and State."

But the kind of flexibility which the Legislative Committee of the Association of American Colleges sought for itself was essentially what was needed in the summer of 1960 if the Congress was to take any positive action. The number of alternative proposals and possible compromises that came up for consideration during the debate and discussion of that summer were far too many and varied and complex to have been settled in advance by the cumbersome techniques of national conventions. The plain fact of the matter was that Washington representatives of higher-education associations could not tell interested Congressional leaders and administrative officials where their memberships stood on each of the possibilities under discussion and did not consider themselves authorized to negotiate in the absence of such positions.

Senator Clark's impatience with the Nation's higher educators became increasingly evident as the summer progressed. Secretary Flemming made it perfectly clear on a number of occasions that this impatience was distinctly bipartisan. Finally, at an American Assembly convened at Arden House in 1960 to discuss relationships between higher education and the Federal Government, Senator Clark gave the educators present what amounted to a "dressing down."

> Politicians should be out in front of the people, I agree. We have a duty of leadership. But we cannot afford to get too far ahead of the people we lead. For if we do, there is great risk we will be shot down from behind on election day.
>
> I wonder whether existing organizations in the field of higher education are set up to do the needed job of working out a proper plan for Federal aid and then lobbying vigorously for it? I suspect that, to some extent, they are immobilized by internal divisions on the basic questions, first, of whether Federal aid in any form is desirable and, second, if so, who should get it? The American Council on Education, the American Association of Land-Grant Colleges and State Universities, the Council for Financial Aid to Education, Inc., the Association of American Colleges, the Association of American Universities, the Council

for the Advancement of Small Colleges, the Association for Higher Education of the National Education Association, and the American Association of Junior Colleges are a rather heterogeneous group to unite on a legislative program. Would it not be desirable to organize an *ad hoc* committee of leading educators and other citizens who are convinced of the need for Federal aid so that, when they meet, they need not argue whether, but only how?

Let us remember that educators are not monks who take a vow of poverty, both for themselves and for the institutions they serve. They, too, are American citizens with the right, indeed the duty, to petition for redress of grievances and to indicate to their elected representatives how they would like those grievances redressed.

At this point, it became abundantly evident to the Washington representatives of higher-education associations that they were in danger of losing the sympathy of influential political leaders in both the Administration and the Congress if they continued to take the position that they could not comment responsively on legislative matters in the absence of approved positions formally adopted by their entire memberships. Making it clear to all concerned that they were not speaking for their associations, a handful of the Washington Executive Secretaries met with Senator Clark's staff and agreed to draft a legislative proposal for Federal assistance in the construction of non-revenue-producing facilities. (They shared Senator Clark's view that revenue-producing facilities should continue to be financed through the existing College Housing Loan Program.) In something less than a week, these able and knowledgeable Executive Secretaries succeeded in drafting a bill which Senator Clark immediately introduced as S. 3776 on June 29, 1960. It provided for direct lump-sum matching grants for the construction of academic facilities, with the option of direct Federal loans (at favorable interest rates) for those institutions that did not choose to accept the direct grants.[10] What their associations and organizations had been unable to work out, these realistic agents had been able to develop almost overnight.

As it all turned out, this unlikely and virtually unprecedented example of mobility on the part of the Executive Secretaries went for nought. The 86th Congress, reconvening after the political conventions of 1960, failed to consider the Clark bill. At the last minute, a "bobtailed" housing bill, which included $500 million for college housing loans but no funds for public housing, passed both Houses of Congress and gave American higher education the one thing that it had clearly wanted and the one thing for which it had worked with unity and vigor. Interestingly enough, and as a further insight into the ways of the Congress, the housing bill was adopted in the closing hours of the 86th Congress by the ingenious device of proposing it as an amendment to a joint resolution giving the Commission to Celebrate the 175th Anniversary of the Declaration of Independence another four months in which to file its final report! There was some reason to believe that as much might have been done for academic facilities had the leading national organizations been able to reach some agreement among themselves, or had they been willing to authorize their spokesmen to negotiate realistically in the heat and pressure of legislative activity.

It remains to be seen whether the efforts of the Executive Secretaries in the closing days of the 86th Congress were "too little and too late." [11] But the recital of the case study does demonstrate certain aspects of the nature of higher-educational organization, and particularly its ability to act on Federal legislative matters, that deserve further attention. Most importantly, it suggests that educators familiar with the ways of the Congress and the realities of political life can act and act effectively when not encumbered by the need to testify that their views have the uniform and wholehearted support of their colleagues.

A basic problem, of course, lies in the apparent assumption that there is such a thing as "American higher education." The notion that some kind of consensus can be achieved among all the persons, organizations, and institutions having an interest in higher education is in itself open to question. Segments of higher education—groups of institutions in higher education of a relatively homogeneous nature—can and do act with great effect on the Washington scene. In 1959, the Association of American Universities, aided by a counsel with a hard-headed awareness of political realities, succeeded in modifying Title I of the Urban Renewal Act, making it possible for an urban community to count toward its local contribution for purposes of matching Federal funds the expenditures of an urban university in campus development. In 1960, the American Association of Land-Grant Colleges and State Universities succeeded in winning a threefold increase in the annual Federal authorizations for instructional funds to their member institutions. This latter was accomplished over the Administration's "objection in principle" to Federal legislation which tended to favor one group of institutions over the interests of all institutions of higher education. Both actions required some political finesse, and both required some substantial (though not extensive) educational support for a specific objective.

The ability of groups of institutions to win Congressional support for their specific needs and objectives is of interest, not only because it suggests that these organizations pack political punch and can, where they have a clear-cut objective, operate effectively in a political context; it is also of interest because no other group of educational institutions interposes a serious complaint or objection. There is a kind of tacit understanding among the several organizations in American higher education that no one of them will openly object to Federal benefits directed toward another group. It is true that the American Association of Land-Grant Colleges and State Universities, a perennial spokesman for low-cost public higher education, has looked askance at proposals for a Federal scholarship program. The Land-Grant Association has not actively opposed such legislation. Similarly, associations of private colleges raised no objection when the Land-Grant Association set out to seek increased Federal appropriations for its instructional purposes; it is entirely possible that they could have blocked legislation if they had. Where one educational association can support legislation that will benefit another, it does; where it cannot support such legislation, it at least remains silent. The workings of this "code" among the several types and groups of institutions contribute to the rather uneven progress of Federal legislation designed to help higher education, and quite probably contribute to the failure of comprehensive legislation designed to assist all institutions.

The code works consistently where like-minded groups of institutions act in their collective interest. Why does it not work when an effort is made to develop a position for all of higher education? Why do obstructing differences of opinion emerge only where the interests of all are concerned?

It cannot be attributed alone to a lack of uniformity within the pluralistic system of higher education. We have observed earlier that organized higher education could not in 1960 seem to agree on a program of aid for the construction of academic facilities. Yet when the American Council on Education polled its members, 90 per cent of those responding favored a dual program of Federal grants and optional loans. Even among the 10 per cent dissenters, a clear majority indicated that they would take advantage of such a program if enacted. Clearly, there existed a striking degree of agreement.

The obstacles in the instance of facilities legislation may suggest the basic nature of the problem. In the first instance, minority-opinion spokesmen exercise an inordinate influence within educational organizations. Whether this is a natural outgrowth of academic tradition or a fault of organization, it is nonetheless true that a small group of objectors were able to forestall national associations from expressing their majority views. The desire for harmony in a number of organizations has caused a clear majority to fall prey to a stubborn, articulate minority. At some point along the road to maturity and effectiveness, organizations learn the difference between consensus and unanimity, between respect for minority views and immobilization by a minority. Educators are not alone in facing this problem, but face it they must.

Another obstacle in the construction-legislation affair that offers insight into a broader problem was the fact that educators assembled in convention could not resist the instinct to speak as statesmen. That may sound cynical, but the fact of the matter is that the very same educators who attested to their need for and interest in Federal assistance when they responded to the aforementioned questionnaire were those who undermined their common interest by questioning its wisdom in the context of public policy. When they debated the possibility of aid to higher education, they were not content to describe their needs and the most effective manner of meeting them; instead, they took on the larger issue, whether it would constitute sound public policy to meet these needs. They did not argue over their needs and interests; they argued over a broad question of public policy, in this instance, the so-called Church-State issue.

What made their Executive Secretaries effective where the leaders of the associations were not may lie in just this area. Instead of trying to agree upon what was good for themselves, educational leaders had presumed to decide what was good for the Nation. What distinguished the national organizations from their Washington representatives and what may distinguish them from national organizations in other walks of American life is that they regard themselves not as a group seeking the assistance of the Government in meeting their needs, but as a group of educators gathered together to mold public safety. Viewed in one light it is a little presumptuous for a group of educators to attempt—as a group—to resolve an issue such as that of Church and State *before* it comes to the Congress. At least, it indicates a lack of awareness of the manner in which the Congress considers the needs of various segments of our society.

The following is an example of the kind of added burden of responsibility assumed by educators in their public roles; it is from an address to the Land-Grant Association convention in 1960:

> . . . if this Association urges either explicitly or implicitly Federal aid for general support of higher education, then it must be prepared to answer most of the above questions of "to whom" and "how."
>
> If we urge the support and that it should extend to *all* types of institutions—to private and church-related as well as to public —then we become advocates of grave departures from established principles in American public policy. These are important principles. We would be saying that general Federal aid to higher education is so urgently needed that the principles must succumb. Do we believe that?
>
> If we urge the support but that it be extended only to presently tax-supported, *publicly* controlled institutions, then we put ourselves somewhat in the role of a "dog in the manger" vis-à-vis the private and church-related institutions and of appearing unconcerned for their welfare.
>
> It is possible that any proposal for general Federal support which did include the non-public colleges and universities would fail of enactment, and equally that one which did *not* include them would fail of enactment.
>
> Sooner or later, however, any group of responsible educators must have an opinion on this problem and express it. That opinion should reflect the most earnest concern for the well-being of our free society and be so soundly grounded as to mark the way for generations.

The key phrase, of course, is ". . . any group of *responsible* educators must have an opinion on this problem and express it." This assumption, voluntarily, of responsibility for the national welfare comes naturally enough to educational leaders, but one wonders whether it could not with equal validity be said that "any group of responsible educators must have an opinion" on every major issue of public policy "and express it." At any rate, this self-imposed sense of corporate responsibility for having and expressing views on issues of public policy has gotten in the way of effective expression of higher-educational needs.

What the Executive Secretaries did *not* do was to attract attention to the issues involved. Their years in Washington had taught them what others may not have understood so clearly, that effective pursuit of one's interests often involves finding ways to avoid broader issues that serve to obstruct action, and never involves raising such issues gratuitously.[12] Every sophisticated college president knows this and applies it in his day-to-day dealings at his institution. As applied to the national scene, however, this guide to action strikes many of these same presidents as smacking of intellectual dishonesty. Perhaps it does, if judged solely against the obligation of the scholar to seek the truth, whatever it might be. That is not their primary obligation when acting as men of affairs, however; and somehow this conflict in perspectives, shown so clearly by the actions of the educational organizations, on the one hand, and the statement by Senator Clark, on the other, will need to be resolved.

THE IMPACT OF FEDERAL PROGRAMS

If the organization of higher education in the United States is confusing—which is not to say confused—at least two things have to be said of it. In the first instance, it is changing, largely through growth, and thus seems especially elusive. In the second place, it must be said that a significant part of the change is inspired by, or results from, the activities of the Federal Government.

The impact of Federal activity on the posture of American higher education is a relatively new field of concern. The lack of thoroughness with which it has been studied should not, however, discourage consideration of those evidences that can be called forth. The interplay of forces between Government and higher education cannot be understood without some discussion of the subject.

Among Institutions

Some of this influence is obvious. The American Association for the Advancement of Science need only be compared with its sister agencies, the American Council of Learned Societies, representing the humanities, and the Social Science Research Council. In terms of staff, budget, organization, and outlook, only one of these bears the unmistakable imprint of Government interest and favor. Only one is located in Washington! The day the American Council of Learned Societies or the Social Science Research Council moves its headquarters to within mortar range of the Capitol, we shall know that a major shift in Federal policy has occurred.

The organization of Land-Grant institutions is probably the most dramatic example of the Federal impact on interinstitutional organization, though the impetus is now ancient history. Their common purpose, as identified by Federal interest and support, has brought these institutions together into what is probably, pound for pound, the most effective educational association on the national scene. Though the individual members of the association now vary widely from one another in virtually every respect, the single fact of their original Federal subvention seems to hold them together. Certainly their unique relationship with the Federal Government has given them a sense of being at home with Federal policy and program issues that contributes to their aggregate effectiveness on the national scene.

Less profound but more obvious effects of Federal impact of a positive nature can be seen in such organizations as the Modern Language Association, whose national influence and organizational stature were enormously enhanced by the language programs authorized in the National Defense Education Act. Deans of the Nation's graduate schools, though loosely organized in a variety of regional groups, have become so much the focus of a variety of

Federal fellowship programs that they created a national organization in 1961, largely in order to achieve representation in Washington! There is evidence that some university presidents disapprove of their graduate deans having their own organization and lobby, which in turn suggests some of the wave effects of Federal influence.

It is worth noting here that operating agencies in the Federal bureaucracy tend to develop close relationships with the groups they serve, assist, or regulate. The frequent contacts between agency officials and their clientele, and the shared interest in a common subject, make this relationship a natural one. Indeed, except as it may interfere with quasi-regulatory and quasi-judicial functions of the agencies, it can be a healthy, mutually enriching relationship.

Often, however, this natural harmony of interests assumes over the years the form of an alliance, with each party having a strong stake in preserving and enhancing the power of the other as a means of doing the same for its own power. There is nothing unnatural in this process, but it does tend to introduce barriers against any attempts to coordinate policy among related agencies or related clientele groups, for each party comes to have an interest in maintaining its independence and draws strength from its counterpart in asserting independence.

To take a simple example of this process in action, it is clear that those who work in the fields of the life sciences have a vital interest in seeing the U.S. Public Health Service grow and flourish as a source of research funds in the future. It is quite likely that any attempt—to be entirely fanciful—to consolidate the entire Federal research program in one agency would be viewed with alarm by toilers in the life-science vineyards, if for no other reason than that such an action would imply the establishment of priorities across the entire spectrum of science and would increase the competition for the research dollar.

These clientele groups, or interests, or lobbies, to use other terms for the same things, clearly have a great impact on Federal policy making. What is frequently overlooked, however, is the fact that these groups have themselves often been brought into being or strengthened by Federal programs. As the Federal Government grows more active in the area of higher education, and particularly as it acts in a categorical or piecemeal fashion, it can be expected to increase the number and variety of such interest groups.

But the tendency of Federal programs to bring about stronger educational organization in those areas supported by Federal programs is not the only impact on the organization of higher education. Sometimes the effect is regarded as disruptive of existing organization and relationships among institutions.

Interstate and intrastate organizations are a case in point. The three regional compact groups in higher education (Western Interstate Commission for Higher Education, The New England Board of Higher Education, and the Southern Regional Education Board) are voluntary groups, one of whose principal objectives is to coordinate the development of higher-education resources in their respective regions. Since they work largely with public institutions, and since State governments are represented in their memberships, it is quite common for their recommendations for coordinated effort to be reflected in State decisions regarding expenditures and the deployment of those expenditures. Federal programs, dealing as they do directly with institutions, tend to bypass these intermediaries and reduce their effectiveness. And what is true of inter-State arrangements is equally true of intra-State arrangements.

To illustrate: A Midwestern State university applied for and received Federal funds with which to expand one of its graduate programs. It acted within its legal rights in doing so, since no State regulation forbade it. Its proposal, judged on its merits, was approved by the Federal agency involved. The institution clearly was entitled to Federal funds authorized for the purpose. But the president of a rival institution objected, saying that an "agreement" existed among the State universities that was contravened by this application and approval. He protested that the Federal Government should not have approved the application, even though the "agreement" had no standing in law and had so little moral force behind it that one of the institutions had felt free to submit its application. The objecting president obviously felt that the Federal Government should have given to an informal agreement substance and standing that it could not claim in its own right. Indeed, he went so far as to describe the Federal action as an unwarranted trespass on State authority. Though the authors regard the criticism itself as unwarranted, the incident does illustrate one of the variety of ways in which Federal actions touch upon tender areas of relationships among colleges and universities.

Within Institutions

What effect has the growing Federal activity in the field of higher education had on the organization of institutions of higher education themselves and on the distribution of power within them?

Actually, very little is known of a systematic nature of the answer to this question. Sadly, academic people—social scientists in particular—have been slow to turn the high-powered tools of their research on the affairs of higher education. Nevertheless, there is a feeling that some important changes in institutional structure are occurring, and the subject is important enough to warrant some speculation on the possible effects of increasing Federal activity.

First, however, there is one development that has been fairly well documented, perhaps because it is so completely visible. It is the development of university-associated laboratories and research centers, operated by one or more universities. These organizations need be considered only briefly here, for one of the causes of their development in the first place was a desire to isolate certain kinds of research activity from the main university campus. Thus, once established, their effect on the operations of the universities involved has been marginal. Indeed, the fact that many of the large research centers are managed by universities is largely the result of the way the mobilization of scientific personnel was handled during World War II. There is no inherent reason why some—like Argonne, Brookhaven, or the University of California's Radiation Laboratory—should be university-managed, while others are not. This is not to say that the schools involved do not derive some benefit from the activity; the Radiation Laboratory provides important research opportunities for graduate students at Berkeley, as an example. However, while it might be more difficult, there is no necessary reason why these benefits could not be derived from some other organizational arrangement.

It should be pointed out, too, that the establishment of a separate research facility can, if improperly managed, have harmful effects on the parent university. It can cause antagonism between the staff of the research unit and the regular university faculty and in some circumstances can produce even more harmful effects. Kidd quotes the following instance as a case in point:

> One of our large universities, with an off-campus activity in a large facility which is being terminated, through its deans and vice-president, deliberately sought a new defense project to keep the faculty and its technical workers busy. After some months a new projected area of technical study having to do directly with warfare was suggested by one of the services, on a fiscal basis rapidly expanding into millions of dollars during the next several years. The university vice-president promptly accepted the contract and then notified the physics, chemistry, and mathematics departments that it was their task to evolve an approach to these war problems. The assignment was accepted with great reluctance by the individuals concerned, but now the university has the expanding contract.[13]

There is no reason to believe that such instances are widespread or that they cannot be avoided by good administration and sound policy guidelines. There is no denying the danger, however, that an organization, once established, can develop a life and force of its own that cause it to outlive its original usefulness and to cast around for new tasks. In the process innocent bystanders can be injured. Two men experienced in such affairs have put the sensible, if ideal, conclusion to the problem: "When duty has been done, the university has no cause to continue in the management of such operations unless it can enhance quality and, at the same time, strengthen educational processes." [14]

As more experience has been gained with the use of special-purpose research installations, there has come an increasing concern over their possible alienation from the academic atmosphere, and a consequent interest in seeing that they are integrated into the spirit of the parent university, and the actual operation where possible. This concern was evidenced by the Seaborg panel of the President's Science Advisory Committee in its 1960 report on basic research and graduate education. The panel recommended that "separate research installations should be avoided whenever possible," and that "new research laboratories for special fields should be attached to universities whenever it is practicable, and universities should make full educational use of such facilities." As the Seaborg panel noted,

> when a new field of interest becomes urgent, there is always temptation to believe that a new and separate research installation is the easy answer. In basic research, at least, such a conclusion is usually questionable, and this temptation should be resisted. As a general rule, such new undertakings should be made working parts of universities—or groups of universities, if the size of the enterprise justifies the additional administrative trouble involved in such joint ventures.

The recommendations of this influential group should have a salutary effect on the thinking of Government agencies about appropriate organizational forms.

While there is no desire to dismiss the formal research center as insignificant, the main burden of this discussion is the network of less formal relationships that have grown up between particular agencies and particular parts of the university community. This is a subject which has produced a good deal of academic folklore and which many people sense to be of real significance. For example, stories are legion of the professor who has a large research grant and, in the course of a dispute with his own university administration, simply leaves his position and takes his research grant, equipment, and graduate students to another institution which will welcome all of them.

When an incident of this sort happens, it can, of course, be most upsetting to the first institution. The basic problem, however, is even more important than such more or less temporary dislocations at a particular school. Put broadly, and put in the form of a question, it is this: "Does the dispersed nature of programs affecting higher education within the Federal Government tend to fragment institutions of higher education and to cause a dispersal of policy-making power within them?"

We suggest that the answer to the question is yes, and that this answer has important implications for institutions of higher education. Effective power in institutions of higher education has traditionally been decentralized. There are, of course, differences among institutions, but on the whole faculties have been quick to sense and ready to resist encroachments by the central administration upon their own rights and prerogatives. Local circumstances, or skillful administration and faculty politics, can smooth over rough areas, but there are few, if any, American colleges or universities characterized by highly centralized power structures.

We should hasten to say that this is not necessarily a bad situation. We have already made the point in another context that centralization of authority, neat lines of command, and tidy administrative arrangements have no inherent virtues that make them obviously better suited to all situations. Indeed, the virtues of decentralization and substantial independence of action commend themselves at least as much in the abstract. Nevertheless, there is a point at which freedom becomes anarchy and the glorification of power dispersed becomes a justification for the failure to plan intelligently.

It is not necessary even to guess whether academic organization has ever neared those perilous points. It is necessary only to point out that policies of the Federal Government have had the effect of encouraging fragmenting tendencies already present in the academic situation.[15] The process involved here is not a complicated one, and it can work at all levels of university organization. The example already given pictured a situation in which an individual faculty member, by virtue of a research grant made to him on the basis of his ability as an investigator, gained substantial power vis-à-vis the institutional administration. It is easy to construct a hypothetical case in which the point at issue between the two was the administration's unwillingness to assign additional space to the research project on the grounds that the space was needed more for some other purpose. Obviously, the point here is not who was right or who was wrong—indeed, it is possible for both to be "right." Rather, it is that the assignment of funds to an individual from an outside agency gave that individual a bargaining weapon not otherwise available with which he could dispute the allocation of university resources—a function reserved in most organizations to a central administrative authority. The policy of the outside agency—quite correct for its own purposes—by which a particular investigator is to do a particular piece of research gave that man a sanction he would not otherwise have had.

Moving away from the level of the individual faculty member and the individual project grant, it is no secret that the close relationship between the U.S. Department of Agriculture and colleges of agriculture gives the latter a degree of autonomy not usually held by other units within a university. It is sometimes claimed, for example, that a degree of specialization made possible, and indeed encouraged, by U.S. Department of Agriculture research funds makes it difficult to integrate agricultural-school faculty into the regular graduate-school instructional program of the university.

Again, it is important to remember that the issue is not one of the importance of the work supported by the U.S. Department of Agriculture funds, but rather of the effect that support has on the institution's ability to plan its educational program as a whole.

To the examples thus far mentioned, there should be added the several Federal matching-grant programs, such as the construction grants for health research facilities administered by the National Institutes of Health. The matching-grant principle has always had a potentially distorting effect by encouraging expenditures—in this case by colleges and universities—for purposes that might not be of the highest priority, were other things equal. Other things are made unequal, of course, by the availability of supporting funds, and so a second-priority project may be undertaken, while the first priority is temporarily shelved. It is difficult, indeed, for an administrator to deny some part of his institution permission to proceed on a project which he knows is needed and for which help is available, even though he knows something else may be needed more. The college president whose priority list has a humanities building at the top and new wing for the medical school near the bottom would be a hard-bitten man indeed if he were to tell his medical school dean he must decline a proffered matching grant for the latter project. But if he does not take this position, an outside source of funds has reached in over his shoulder and reshuffled his priorities. It should not be overlooked that in a sense this is precisely the purpose of such grant-in-aid programs. They are designed to encourage expenditures for items deemed to be in the national interest by offering to share the cost. It is, always has been, and no doubt always will be a persuasive argument; but it nonetheless frequently seems like arm twisting to the institution.

It should be clear by now that we are not arguing that such activities on the part of the Federal Government are improper or unwise. On the contrary, it should be equally clear that, at this point in the Nation's development, someone has to set national priorities. The growing complexity of the society and the increasing inability of any single part of it to see national needs and to move to meet them have inexorably moved the burden of those tasks to the Federal Government, not only in education but in other areas as well.

These facts, however, make it all the more important to assess carefully the policies and procedures of the Federal Government and to account for their implications and consequences. The fragmentation of decision-making power within institutions caused by the dispersal of power over educational programs and policies within the Government is one such set of consequences, and it is incumbent upon interested persons to recognize and deal with them.

As an aspect of this general problem, it is worth noting that policies of individual Federal agencies, as distinct from the sum total of all agency actions, may have the effect of gathering power together within institutions to an extent that had not been possible before. An example of this process is found in a feature of the National Defense Graduate Fellowship Program. Any institution that offers, or wishes to offer, a doctor's degree is eligible to apply, and it may submit applications for as many of its graduate programs as it wishes. Each application on its face represents an area of graduate work which the institution wants to move forward, but obviously there are some things any well-ordered university would rather do before it does others. As we have already suggested, it is often difficult for the central authority to resist pressure from an individual professor or department if some funds are made available from outside of the institution to support the faculty member's or department's plans. The National Defense Fellowship Program then would have the capacity to aggravate this tendency further, if it were not for the fact that graduate schools submitting applications are asked to rank in order of priority all the proposals being submitted and to submit them in the name of the university. The rating allows a central authority within the institution to indicate priorities to a Federal agency. The fact that a good deal of concern has been shown thus far to keep these ratings confidential indicates that the ratings are taken seriously and are in fact being used in some places as a means of keeping under control departments that are viewed as having a reach exceeding their grasp. To be more precise, it may be difficult for a dean to say to a disappointed department chairman, "I don't think you ought to undertake a Ph.D. program." It is much easier for all concerned if the dean can say instead, "Those people in Washington won't give us the money for your Ph.D. program." Whoever in the institution has the responsibility for establishing these priorities—and it is usually the graduate dean—has his powers strengthened and his control over the course of his institution enlarged.

In dealing with the Federal Government, universities are faced not only with the prospect of handling a variety of agencies, each making its claim on institutional resources, but each institution must find ways of organizing and controlling its contacts with any single agency. For the truth of the matter is that almost any Federal program touches a university at a number of different points. A sponsored research program, for example, will in one way or another involve not only faculty, students, and departmental chairmen, but the graduate dean, the financial or business officer, the registrar, and physical-plant director as well. It touches in such a variety of places within the institution that it poses a sizable problem of coordination—frequently made more complicated by the fact that the institution is asked at some points to apply standards not of its own making. In any large university the points of impingement and the number of people involved can be multiplied by the number of Federal programs in which the institution participates. The result will be some indication of the administrative complexity which the growing number and variety of Federal activities impose on an institution of higher education. Perhaps the total effect is most clearly measured by the "indirect cost" charges levied by institutions on Federal contracts and grants—and by the vigor with which the institutions insist upon full payment of these related costs.

It is little wonder that, faced with an increasingly complex array of Government programs, which greatly complicates campus administration and which gives added impetus to the normal centripetal forces which operate on a campus, the universities have themselves developed new administrative devices. A new figure is appearing on many campuses. He may be called the coordinator of research, or the director of government and foundation relations, or by any of a variety of other titles. His essential job, however, is to try to bring together in one place the contracts which the university has with the Government and other outside agencies. It is impossible to generalize in any meaningful way about the powers and duties of the office. In one place, it may be simply a clearinghouse for paper work; in another, it may be responsible for screening, evaluating, and passing judgment on requests by faculty for outside support; and in still another, a major part of the office may consist of soliciting funds by advertising the university's resources to granting agencies.

One of the functions that might most profitably be performed by this new figure in university hierarchies—though it is hardly a job for one man—would be to assess the extent to which his institution has surrendered control of its own fate and future as a result of complex involvement in outside programs. A leading American educator already has warned that universities are in danger of becoming academic supermarkets, implying a kind of other-directed willingness to sell whatever there may be a demand—and a price—for. Certainly Federal programs in complex, research-oriented universities have now reached the point where careful study should be given to their total impact on the institution and their net effect upon its essential autonomy.[16]

NOTES

[1] The Association of American Colleges, the Association of American Universities, the Catholic Educational Association, the National Association of State Universities, the American Association of University Professors, the Association of American Agricultural Colleges and Experiment Stations, the National Education Association, and several other similar organizations and associations joined together in this effort.

[2] While for the purposes of this discussion it is important principally to consider the activities of the Council as they relate to Federal activities, it is necessary to acknowledge the Council's broader function for one reason at least. It is important for the Council, as a research and study organization, to enjoy the privilege of receiving gifts and grants which are deductible for income tax purposes. Partly because it enjoys this tax-exempt privilege, the American Council annually receives some $2 million in grants and contracts for general support and special projects. The Internal Revenue Service of the Treasury Department extends tax-exempt privileges of this sort to organizations only if, among other things, it can be assured that no substantial part of the organization's program and activities consist of lobbying before the Congress of the United States. Herein lies a problem of the American Council on Education. Founded originally to represent higher-education interest vis-à-vis the Federal Government, and having reached a degree of political sophistication that suggests that lobbying is vital to those interests, it nonetheless finds that it has grown to a point in terms of the breadth of its non-Federal activities where it must be careful of its lobbying in order to retain its privileged tax status.

[3] Though it is by no means the only one. During the last ten years the following committees of the Council have come into being to treat with aspects of Federal relationships: Committee on Taxation and Fiscal Reporting, Committee on Institutional Projects Abroad, Commission on Education and International Affairs, Committee on Sponsored Research, Committee on Television, and Committee on Urban Renewal.

[4] The American Council on Education's heavy reliance upon broad consensus was stressed by retiring President Arthur S. Adams in his

valedictory address to the Council on October 6, 1960. He said in part: "Your Council is a representative body, constantly devoted to educational achievement by many educational organizations and institutions. To accomplish broad common purposes requires that all of the constituents of the Council be informed about the issues, be alert to the considerations not only of themselves but also of others, and have reached judgments on which all are prepared to act in concert. I am sure you will agree that this all takes time. Yet I am persuaded that this is the only approach on which we can depend for constructive action."

[5] The American Association of Land-Grant Colleges and State Universities, Association of American Universities, Association of American Colleges, State Universities Association, American Association of University Professors, American Society for Engineering Education, Association for Higher Education, American Association of Junior Colleges, National Catholic Education Association, American Association of Colleges of Teacher Education, convened at the American Council on Education. Another quotation from the background document suggests both the purposes of the seminar and some of the weaknesses of present mechanisms:*"What, then, should be the functions of the seminar?* The seminar should, first of all, be *informative.* Representatives of the Council should present all the available background on each issue; representatives of the other organizations should present all the relevant information about positions formally taken by their groups and the reasons supporting them. Second, the seminar should *attempt to reach consensus* on a position commanding maximum support, and should frame recommendations to the appropriate Council committee if necessary. Third, the seminar should explore methods by which organizations can *spread information to their members* and, at appropriate times, *urge their members to act."*

[6] One experienced university president has ventured this analysis, which assumes that the legislative seminar approach will find its way into the continuing operations of the Council: "It will become a sounding board for the constituent members and give them an opportunity formally to influence the program of the Council in ways not now possible. This may make the task of the Committee on Relationships more difficult; on the other hand, it may make it easier because obviously the voices of the constituent members will be stronger than the voices of the individuals on the Committee on Relationships."

[7] The National Academy of Sciences is, of course, a quasi-govern-

mental organization. Its long existence suggests the extent to which fusion of government and nongovernment has been accepted in certain areas, especially the sciences. In January of 1960, Dr. Arthur Bestor urged the extension of the quasi-governmental-foundation concept into the areas of the humanities and social sciences. His advocacy and the expressed opposition of New York State Commissioner James Allen both appear in a release issued by Health, Education, and Welfare Secretary Arthur S. Flemming on January 13, 1961.

[8] These fears were inspired in part by the reaction of Congressional staff who reacted negatively to feelers early in the Second Session of the 86th Congress from higher-education representatives. As is not infrequently the case, aides to Congressional leaders were apparently a good deal more cautious about the issue than were their employers.

[9] The three approaches were hardly compatible in one piece of legislation. Nor were the choices among them easy, however clear-cut the methods in principle. Higher-education spokesmen were profoundly suspicious that the Administration proposal, however earnestly conceived by the Department of Health, Education, and Welfare, was being used by the Administration as a device to abolish the College Housing Loan Program. Thus, they feared that any support of this one approach to financing academic facilities would undermine what was to them the ideal method of financing residential facilities. The choices were further colored, of course, by loyalties to Congressional leaders whose support had been won for earlier positions and programs. This was especially true of the jurisdictional question certain to arise if the Education Committees of the House and Senate acted in any way to affect the College Housing Loan Program, a pet prerogative of the Committees on Banking and Currency.

[10] This latter option paralleled the so-called "Baptist amendment" to the Hill-Burton Hospital Construction Program, under which organizations opposed to the principle of direct Federal grants for church-related hospitals could elect instead to borrow Federal money for the purpose.

[11] The experience of 1961, though highly promising, was inconclusive. The impressive degree of unanimity in support of a program of Federal grants and loans for the construction of academic facilities (largely achieved in the aftermath of the 1960 experience) clearly had its impact on Congress. Despite the fact that the Administration had recommended only loans for the purpose, the harmonious testimony of all higher-education witnesses persuaded the House Committee on

Education and Labor to vote out a combination grant and loan bill with considerable bipartisan support. The eruption of controversies largely centering around other educational legislation stymied efforts to bring the bill to a vote, but the positive response of the House Committee was itself an eloquent testimonial to the united front in higher education.

[12] They could not avoid the issue, of course. The Church-State issue arises unavoidably in any legislative proposal, because private institutions are either eligible or not, and either way someone's views are offended. By including the private institutions but suggesting a grant or loan option, the Executive Secretaries raised the issue in its least alarming form. Nobody was offended in a bread-and-butter sense, and those whose principles might have been offended were assuaged by the questionable inference that the loans were for church-related institutions. The Commission on Legislation of the Association of American Colleges subsequently described the appeal of the proposal in this way: "We cannot imagine any other solution of the problem that would command as wide a measure of agreement as this one. It excludes nobody from aid and compels nobody to accept aid in a form that violates his convictions. It allows each institution to obtain such aid as it may desire in whichever form is better suited to its own circumstances and its own policies."

[13] M. A. Tuve, "Technology and National Research Policy," *Bulletin of Atomic Scientists*, No. 9, p. 291 (1953), quoted in Charles V. Kidd, *American Universities and Federal Research* (Cambridge, Mass., 1959), pp. 181–182.

[14] James McCormack and Vincent A. Fulmer, "Federal Sponsorship of University Research," in *The Federal Government and Higher Education* (Englewood Cliffs, N.J., 1960), p. 93.

[15] One student of the subject has observed that "There is a striking similarity in the organization (or lack of it) of federal agencies and programs and the organization of complex universities. . . . This condition defies organization at either place—university or government—since the essence of many federal programs is assistance to individual investigators, and only incidentally to their institutions. If institutions, as such, are to be helped, the assistance must go to the institutions."

[16] It should be added that at the time of this writing several significant efforts are under way. President Nathan Pusey's announcement that Harvard would undertake such a self-study coincided with

efforts of the U.S. Office of Education, on the one hand, and the Carnegie Corporation, on the other, to encourage such case-study evaluation through grants and contracts. The findings of such studies are certain to be illuminating and likely to suggest changes of policy at both the institutional and Federal levels.

CHAPTER FOUR

THE ISSUES

Introduction

The present educational policies of the Federal Government—and no doubt those for the future as well—are the product of changing circumstances knitted to old habits of mind and action. They are developed in the context of a political, social, and economic system that determines in large measure the shape of those policies. They are tempered, too, by attitudes toward education and toward the proper uses of Federal power that are as old as the Constitution and as current as the nearest Presidential election or the next impressive feat of some other nation's educational system. The Federal interest in education, generally, and in higher education, specifically, can never be viewed as an isolated phenomenon; it is not in the nature of the governmental process that "education" can be abstracted from the rest of the society and dealt with in isolation. Instead, and to the distress of the purist, "noneducational" influences inevitably become involved when Federal educational policy is at stake.

There is no remedy for this state of affairs, unless it be for the Government to remove itself entirely from the educational scene. Since, in some areas, such as the support and purchase of research, this is now impossible, and in other areas, such as the support of students, it is highly unlikely, we are faced with the prospect of either understanding and finding ways to deal with these "noneducational" considerations or of winding up in a hopeless muddle. For sensible people the former is clearly preferable to the latter. Therefore it is necessary to take stock of issues arising from those influences that have been in the past, and certainly will be in the future, a part of any consideration of Federal policies toward higher education. Chief among these are the issues of Church-State relations, Federal control of education, and segregation of the races.

A discussion of these issues as they affect Federal policy, though, might well be misleading were it not prefaced by a few words about the nature of public policy issues generally. In the political arena—and in broad terms it is that which concerns us here—appearance is difficult to separate from reality. The mask may become so much a part of the face that the mask is taken for, and in fact becomes, the face for all practical purposes.

In some cases this fact of public life is harmless and is given tolerant, if bemused, approval. For example, when a man makes his formal announcement that he is a candidate for election to the office for which he has been campaigning publicly for the last two years, everyone smiles and accepts the announcement as part of the game. No harm has been done, after all.

In other cases, however, this confusion of appearance with reality can be harmful, for it can serve to obstruct from public view underlying issues and, thus, inhibit free and full debate. For example, a heavy weapon in the arsenal of opponents of Federal activity is the argument that States' rights must be preserved. The States' rights position has deep roots in American folklore, and it is used as a weapon in a variety of battles, ranging from integration of the schools to the fluoridation of water. Whatever substance the issue has on its own merits, it is clear that it serves in many cases to mask other issues that are never brought into the open— economic self-interest, as an example—and the emotional charge which it carries inhibits discussion of other serious issues of public policy that may be involved in the measure in question.

To a degree—and the precise amount varies from case to case—the triumvirate of issues which concern us here is of a piece with the States' rights position. Each of the three is an issue of substance on which honest men can and do have honest differences. At the same time each is to a degree a stalking horse disguising other motives for support or opposition to a measure.

It is important to understand the dual nature of these issues, for failure to do so can lead to grievous errors of judgment. Such a failure, for example, leads sober people to bemoan the inability of the Congress to consider education measures on their own merits, uncontaminated by such "extraneous" issues as segregation. The view of the relationship between educational policy and segregation that this attitude represents, however, is certain to confuse the issues even further, for it fails to take into account the extent to which segregation is *really* involved in Federal decisions on education and the extent to which it is a fanciful issue used to disguise others. The distinction is crucially important, both as a matter of tactics in meeting opposition and as a question of sound public policy. For failure to recognize substantive issues is as great a political sin as is the effort to obscure them by laying a false scent.

One further point should be made here. In a very real sense, an "issue" in public affairs is whatever people think is an issue. Regardless of how inappropriate or irrelevant a given factor may seem to be, if it is sufficiently important to a large enough number of people to influence their behavior, then it must be dealt with. Maybe it ought not to be important, and maybe the fact that it is important is proof of public irrationality, but history is strewn with the dashed hopes of those who were so taken with the world as it ought to have been that they neglected the world as it was.

The issues with which this section deals are thought by many people to be significant, indeed controlling, in determining Federal policy toward higher education. In addition, these issues are used by other people to disguise quite different motives. On both counts they are worth our consideration, for on both they are certain to influence the future relationship between the Federal Government and higher education.

CHURCH AND STATE

In September of 1789, the First Congress of the United States passed by the necessary number, and submitted to the States, a Resolution containing 12 proposed amendments to the new Constitution. The preamble to the Resolution said, "The conventions of a number of the States having at the time of their adopting the Constitution, expressed a desire, in order to prevent misconstruction or abuse of its powers, that further declaratory and restrictive clauses should be added, and as extending the ground of public confidence in the government will best insure the beneficent ends of its institution. . . ."

By December 15, 1791, three-fourth of the States had ratified 10 of the 12 proposals, and on that day the Bill of Rights was officially added to the Constitution. The first words of the First Amendment are, "Congress shall make no law respecting an establishment of religion, or prohibiting the free exercise thereof; . . . ."

There are few strains of American thought that go deeper or have stronger roots than that which has to do with the separation of Church and State. Every American believes in it; no American would be guilty of doing anything purposely to subvert it. The "wall of separation between Church and State", made famous by Jefferson in his letter to the Danbury Baptists, is a firm part of the American tradition. It is one thing, however, to win agreement on a broad principle—no doubt, even the Russians would stand with us in defense of virtue, so long as the ingredients were not specified —it is quite another to win the same consensus on the working details of the principle. Thus, after almost 175 years, there is no clear agreement about the meaning of those seemingly simple words. Dispute over them raises the bile of otherwise reasonable men, and that most august and austere of American institutions, the Supreme Court, has been reduced to such a state that an eminent Justice concluded his bitter dissent in a First Amendment case with this comment on the opinion of the majority of his brethren: "Today's judgment will be more interesting to students of psychology and of the judicial processes than to students of constitutional law."

Indeed, few issues in recent years have produced such sharply divided opinion on the Court as that of the application of the First Amendment to education. It is worth emphasizing that the differences are not over the principle of the First Amendment, to which all adhere, but over its application in fact. The past fifteen years have seen opinion on the Court range across a wide spectrum of views. In *Everson v. Board of Education*,[1] Justice Black wrote the majority opinion which held that it was not a violation of the First Amendment for the State of New Jersey to reimburse parents for the cost of their children's transportation to and from a parochial school. At the same time, however, he gave to the principle of the First Amendment a most sweeping interpretation:

> The "establishment of religion" clause of the First Amendment means at least this: Neither a State nor the federal government can set up a church. Neither can pass laws which aid one religion, aid all religions, or prefer one religion over another. . . . In the words of Jefferson, the clause against establishment of religion by law was intended to erect a wall of separation between Church and State.

Justice Rutledge, dissenting, saw the constitutional meaning in precisely the same way and applied it with directly opposite results. He said:

> The Constitution requires, not comprehensive identification of state with religion, but complete separation. . . . Two great drives are constantly in motion to abridge, in the name of education, the complete division of religious and civil authority

which our forefathers made. One is to introduce religious education and observance into the public schools. The other, to obtain public funds for the aid and support of various private religious schools. . . . In my opinion both avenues were closed by the Constitution.

In the second so-called "released-time" cases, *Zorach v. Clauson*,[2] representing the first of the "great drives" seen by Justice Rutledge, Justice Douglas, with as much devotion to the principle of separation, nevertheless saw it in quite a different light. He said:

> We are a religious people whose institutions presuppose a Supreme Being. We guarantee freedom to worship as one chooses. . . . We sponsor an attitude on the part of government that shows no partiality to any one group. . . . When the state encourages religious instruction or cooperates with religious authorities by adjusting the schedule of public events to sectarian needs, it follows the best of our traditions. For it then respects the religious nature of our people and accommodates the public service to their spiritual needs. . . . Government may not finance religious groups nor undertake religious instruction nor blend secular and sectarian education. . . . But we find no constitutional requirement which makes it necessary for government to be hostile to religion.

Fortunately, it is no part of our task here to determine whether the First Amendment merely prohibits the establishment of a State church; or whether it requires the Government simply to remain neutral in sectarian matters, while allowing relations on an even-handed basis with all sects; or whether it proscribes entirely any relations between the Government and religion in any context. These brief quotations, however, serve to give the flavor of this controversy on what is presumably its loftiest plane. Much of the emotional content which so charges the issue in the local, State, and national political arenas is filtered out in the rarer air of the

Supreme Court chamber; enough remains, however, to suggest the potential divisiveness of the dispute. Our goal here is to suggest the relevance of the Church-State issue to higher education and to examine its past and possible future impact.

In point of fact, the Church-State controversy has never infected relations between the Federal Government and higher education in quite the same way and with nearly the same impact as it has when elementary and secondary schools have been involved; that is to say, it has less often been the subject of open dispute. Its influence has been felt in the shaping of programs so as to avoid dispute, rather than overt contention over the application of the principle of separation of Church and State. There are several important reasons for this. First, as we have already seen, Federal programs affecting higher education have, on the whole, been narrowly drawn as to purpose, if not scope; that is to say, they are for the most part programs in which the Government buys research, supports individual students, or lends money for a narrow class of objects. Indeed, as we have suggested, legislation is sometimes framed in such ways just so that the First Amendment controversy might be avoided. Still, the fact is that when the Government is acting in the role of purchaser, it may purchase from whoever can supply the product. Similarly, when money is given to a student so that he may pursue his studies, no First Amendment question is raised if he happens to decide to go to Notre Dame.

Obviously, both of these examples involve a slight fiction. In the one the institution has received some benefits from a research grant or contract, and in the other it may well have been enabled to get a better student than it would have if that student were not receiving Government aid. Nevertheless, since the purpose of the latter program is to aid students and not to support institutions, the benefit to a religious institution is sufficiently indirect to avoid controversy.

A second reason for the more muted tones of the dispute in

the area of higher education is that there is nothing in higher education analogous to the universal and free system of public education existing at the lower levels. The great and growing role now played by State and municipal universities is a fairly recent development in the history of higher education. Indeed, private institutions, although not all church-related, still account for roughly 40 per cent of the total college enrollment and closer to half the degrees granted each year. This contrasts with the fact that only some 14 per cent of elementary and secondary school pupils are enrolled in nonpublic schools. If one can conceive, at all, of higher education without privately supported schools, that conception can only be one of limited opportunities and inadequate resources.

The fact is that society *needs* private higher education in a much more direct and tangible way than it needs private elementary and secondary schools. This is especially true since, as we have seen, Federal interest has traditionally been related to national needs for highly trained manpower or some equally compelling educational product. Awareness of this fact lends a measure of balance to discussions of higher education that is lacking elsewhere.

Finally, there is a difference between the school and college situations, the implications of which are hard to assess but certainly of significance. It is that younger children are involved in the grade schools and that this injects an emotional element that is not present in discussions of higher education. Obviously, too, the public school situation has in it an element of compulsion. Children, after all, are required to attend school, and so constitute a truly captive audience.

Therefore, the emotionalism which so marks disputes at the grade school level is not present in higher education. The following dialogue between Representative Peter Frelinghuysen (R., N.J.) and Dr. Stanley Lowell, Methodist minister and Associate Director of Protestants and Other Americans United for Separation of Church and State, taken from testimony on a Federal scholarship program held before the House Education Committee, sums up the difference:

> MR. FRELINGHUYSEN: Why is it that you are not opposed to grants to students in sectarian colleges and you would be opposed to them in education at a lower level?
>
> MR. LOWELL: For several reasons, Mr. Chairman. I suppose the better one being that the actual sectarian tie at the level of higher education is much more ethereal than at the lower level. There are many colleges which are nominally sectarian but, actually, when one examines their control, it is only a nominal relationship; whereas, the schools at the lower level dealing as they do with younger and more impressionable children have, as a rule, a tighter sectarian control, and we think there is quite a substantial difference in that respect.

If we may put it this way, there is, at the grade school level, little more in the Church-State issue than meets the eye, while in higher education there is a good deal more. By this we mean that the manifestations, implications, and effects of the issue are generally open to view at the lower levels, but are hidden beneath a seemingly placid surface at the higher level.

The form which the Church-State issue takes in higher education is suggested by the following proposition: The closer to a program of general educational assistance a proposal is, the more likely it is to stir up the Church-State controversy.

From this proposition we can understand some past actions and perhaps divine some future developments. In part, as we have already seen, the fact that so much Federal activity in higher education is of a special-purpose character is due in turn to the fact that so many Federal agencies have special purposes to serve. Much of this kind of activity, developed during and after World War II, and its association with national emergencies, immediate and prospective, served to suppress potentially damaging disputes.

Starting in about 1950, however, and running parallel to this first group of programs, there has come an increasing drive toward Federal legislation that would treat institutions of higher education in their primary capacity rather than as appendages to the national defense establishment. It is in this group of proposals and programs —for example, college housing loans, some aspects of the National Defense Education Act, the proposed academic facilities building program—that the Church-State issue begins to appear. It appears in various ways and in different guises, but its presence is evident to the discerning observer. In general, the potentially divisive character of the issue has been avoided by the creation of a number of polite fictions which allow the substance of the legislation to be considered without too much argument over its implications for the separation of Church and State. Such adjustments are not made without a price being exacted somewhere. Sometimes the price has been the excision of program elements that could not be covered by the agreed-on fictions, and at other times the price has been the setting of precedents that encumber future action. Some examples will help make this point clearer.

The College Housing Loan Program rests on two debatable propositions which are now part of its structure. The first is that, since the program is for assistance in the construction of non-academic facilities, it should not be considered as a program in aid of education, but rather as a housing program. The second is that a loan is not an aid to education—and hence religion—whereas a grant is.

Both of these are fairly transparent disguises—imagine the ordinary college or university without dormitories—but both have been remarkably successful in doing the job for which they were designed. In particular, the loan device has been most serviceable as a means of avoiding thorny First Amendment questions. The underlying assumption is that a loan which must be repaid does not constitute aid or support to a religious institution. So widely held is this view that Baptist groups that would not accept grants under the Hill-Burton Hospital Construction Program asked the

Congress to attach a loan provision to the Program so that their people might also contribute to solving the hospital-shortage problem. The result is now frequently referred to as "the Baptist amendment."

The difference between a loan and a grant, however, seems to become one of degree rather than kind when the loan is made at interest rates lower than those available in the private money market and with repayment terms more generous than ordinarily available. The latter may be what makes the loan at all feasible for the borrower, and the former is little more or less than a dollar subsidy.

As we have said, there is nothing inherently wrong with such fictions. Indeed, in cases like the one just cited, they allow implementation of what a majority feel to be desirable social policy by providing an honorable way to avoid a contentious issue. The difficulty is that ruses good for one set of circumstances may not be good for—indeed, may be positively obstructive to—another set. Thus, it is fairly clear that, while loans are workable for revenue-producing facilities, they are not nearly so useful for such items as classrooms, libraries, and laboratories. In addition, there is simply no way of arguing that such structures are in any way non-educational.

Having sold these propositions in the one, though, it is hard to avoid them in the other. The frustrations that result are implicit in the following statement by Senator Wayne Morse, who was arguing for a loan program for private elementary and secondary school construction:

> For 10 years the college housing program has gone forward successfully. . . . It applies to church colleges and universities of many denominations. I know of no instance where a question has been raised as to the constitutionality of including private—and church—colleges in the loan program for dormitories. Apparently it is all right to provide a place for them to sleep, but not a place for them to learn.

A second example of the uses of illusion in separating education from religion is the shape of several parts of the National Defense Education Act. This is an especially instructive case, for the National Defense Education Act may prove to be the base on which broader-scale Federal action will be built in the future. The program of student loans set up by the Act is one case in point. In brief, the program provides for the establishment of loan funds at Colleges and universities—virtually all are eligible—with a Federal contribution of nine-tenths of the amount of each fund. Loans are made by the schools to their students. The conditions of the loans do not concern us here, except that up to one-half of a loan will be forgiven if a student becomes a full-time teacher in a *public* elementary or secondary school.

Trying to decide what the Congress really meant as opposed to what it actually said is an intoxicating but intellectually dangerous pastime, and we do not intend to indulge in it here. It is quite clear, however, that the logic of the Student Loan Program of the National Defense Education Act is that the actual loans are made to individuals, with the colleges acting more or less as disbursing agents. Hence, it is alleged that no aid to religion is involved when a church-supported school participates, though the Act seems to say that if the student who has borrowed money decides to teach in a sectarian elementary or secondary school, to cancel part of his loan would constitute an aid to the religious group which operated the school. The fiction involved is obvious, for there can be no doubt that a program which enables the school to attract and hold students with long-term, low-interest loans is an aid to most institutions.

Equally interesting, however, is the fact that the Congress was unwilling to take a step that approached aid to private elementary and secondary schools, in spite of the fact that the same principle which sustained inclusion of private colleges applies just as neatly to loan cancellation for teaching in a private school, namely, assistance to an individual, regardless of his choice of school, or in this case, place of employment.

The National Defense Graduate Fellowship Program provides a particularly instructive example of legislative maneuver to avoid the Church-State problem. The original proposal for assistance to graduate education put forward by the Eisenhower Administration called for grants to graduate schools on a matching basis. The purpose of the proposal was to help schools start or expand graduate programs, and they could use the money for any objects toward that end, including fellowships, faculty salaries, books, and laboratory equipment.

If there is one policy matter on which virtually all educators agree, it is that the best of all Federal programs would be one that allotted money to schools to be used in any way each school thought best. The Administration proposal, although limited to the expansion of graduate programs, came close to that ideal by allowing virtually free institutional choice in deciding the best ways to effect that expansion.

The proposal, however, was clearly a grant-in-aid, and since it was to be made available to all schools—public and private, church-related and not—it raised the controversy in unavoidable terms. The proposal never reached the floor of either House of Congress. Instead, it was rewritten in the House Committee and emerged as a program of fellowship aid to individual students. Accompanying each fellowship was a payment to the institution in which the fellow enrolled which would cover *that portion of the cost of starting or expanding a graduate program that was attributable to the fellow.*

The objective of the program had not changed; it remained that of enlarging graduate school facilities in order to train more college teachers. What had changed was the directness with which that goal was to be reached. Most educators would argue that the original proposal would have been more direct, more effective, and educationally sounder. Rather than risk an open debate on the Church-State question, with the attendant danger that the whole Act might be lost, the Congress chose to clothe the program in the garments of student aid, with a payment for cost attached to it. All schools could participate, and a potentially damaging controversy was side-stepped.

Ironically, the question of aid to religion did arise in the administration of the fellowship program, but in a wholly unexpected way, a way that did not at all involve the formula that smoothed the way for enactment of the program. The issue arose, rather, because of awards made to students for the graduate study of religion. Although these awards were for the study of religion as a scholarly discipline, and not as a vocation, they evidently came too close to a line which, however difficult to locate with precision, was discernible on Congressional radarscopes. As a result, the Senate Committee on Labor and Public Welfare proposed in 1961 that the National Defense Education Act be amended to read, "No fellowship shall be awarded to any individual under this title for study at a school or department of divinity or religion, or awarded to an individual for study in religious or theological subjects."

These few examples should suffice to show the ways in which the Church-State issue has been dealt with in the recent past. It should be understood that it is not our intention to debunk or otherwise to attack the methods that have been adopted to meet— or avoid—the issue. In an important sense these methods have worked; that is, they have made possible the establishment of Federal programs that have been of real importance to higher education. In a broader sense, it is surely true that no society—in the world, at least—has ever been able to afford the luxury of facing squarely all the issues that divide its people. The use of fiction as an instrument of cohesion is an indispensable social tool.

What of the future, though? As the drive toward broader Federal programs, clearly in support of higher education, increases— as it surely will—can the issue still be avoided; will the fictions still be serviceable? Our answer to the question may reflect a lack of faith in political ingenuity, but we should say that the issue of aid to religion will be increasingly more difficult to avoid because of the growing drive toward broad support programs. How, then, can the issue be met?

One answer to the question, for which there is a good deal of support, was given to the Council of Presidents of the Association of Land-Grant Colleges and State Universities by John T. Caldwell, now Chancellor of North Carolina State College:

> My own conclusions are offered in the context of what in my opinion is good for our free society over the long pull. They are as follows:
>
> 1. Federal aid to higher education is necessary if this Nation is to realize its full potential in the human community.
>
> 2. Federal aid, as all public tax-based support, should be expended *only* in institutions established, supported and controlled through the constituted organs of civil government.
>
> 3. In addition to general aid so directed, special support to overcome lags in graduate level disciplines could still be encouraged as at present, leaving the general aid to be merged with other institutional resources for flexible, efficient and wise use.
>
> 4. That this Association should take a clear position in support of sound public policy, which is consistent with the historic commitments of our Nation to the principle of separation of church and state, and against the use of public revenues for privately determined ends.[3]

It is surely difficult not to support "sound public policy, which is consistent with the historic commitments of our Nation." The trouble, as we have seen, is that in practice it is not at all clear what those commitments consist of. Thus, another view of the future was given recently in the context of a State system of higher education by the Committee on Higher Education of the State of New York. In its report to the Governor, the Committee noted, ". . . the bulwark of higher education in New York State for many years has been our private colleges and universities, and the great tradition of meeting the need for higher education through a combination of private and public institutions must be preserved for the future." [4]

The Committee then proposed "that the State help to insure the continuance of their effectiveness by inaugurating a program of direct aid to private colleges and universities." [5] The Committee recognized a question as to the constitutional status of direct aid to church-related schools, but urged that "should there be a delay in settling this matter for sectarian institutions, this should not prevent the drawing up of the contracts with non-sectarian colleges and universities." [6]

Still a third statement of the nature of this issue as it is likely to apply to higher education in the future is available. Early in the First Session of the 87th Congress, the Department of Health, Education, and Welfare produced, at the request of Senator Wayne Morse, a comprehensive analysis of the Church-State issue as it applies to education. The conclusions stated on the subject of higher education are most illuminating, coming as they did from an Administration that was highly sensitive to the general issue. The HEW memorandum read, in part:

> This memorandum has discussed first amendment principles, relevant judicial decisions, and criteria for determining the constitutionality of specific legislative proposals all in the context of elementary and secondary education. Since proposals are currently being advanced in the field of higher education, it is appropriate to give consideration to the significantly different context in which any constitutional problem concerning these proposals might arise.
>
> The constitutional principles involved are obviously the same whether the subject is elementary and secondary school education or higher education, but the factual circumstances surrounding the application of the principles are dramatically different. The reasons are largely historical. . . .
>
> There are thus important differences between school and college, not only in terms of history and tradition but also in

terms of the compulsory nature of attendance. There are differences, too, from the standpoint of the national interest involved. At the college and graduate levels the public institutions alone could not begin to cope with the number of young men and women already in pursuit of higher education, and expansion of these institutions or the creation of new ones sufficient to meet the expected increase of enrollment is out of the question. The effort which it is agreed must now be made in the field of higher education would, if confined to public institutions, force an evermore intensive selection of students and evermore concentrated effort to guide them into fields of study deemed important to the national defense and welfare. It would likely induce these institutions to overemphasize particular fields of study to the detriment of a balanced curriculum. Such warping of our educational policies is not to be contemplated lightly, and, to the extent that Congress finds it appropriate to encourage expansion of our university and college facilities, Congress must be free to build upon what we have, the private as well as the public institutions.

All these considerations indicate that aid to higher education is less likely to encounter constitutional difficulty than aid to primary and secondary schools. The same considerations apply even more forcefully to graduate and specialized education. . . .

Loans for construction of facilities may be less constitutionally vulnerable than grants for the same purposes. But this distinction is not here the only one or perhaps even the crucial one. More important are the distinctive factors present in American higher education: the fact that the connection between religion and education is less apparent and that religious indoctrination is less pervasive in a sectarian college curriculum; the fact that free public education is not available to all qualified college students; the desirability of maintaining the widest possible choice of colleges in terms of the student's educational needs in a situation no longer limited by the necessity of attending schools located close to home; the extent to which particular skills can be imparted only by a relatively few insti-

tutions; the disastrous national consequences in terms of improving educational standards which could result from ex-
clusion of, or discrimination against, certain private institutions
on grounds of religious connection; and the fact that, unlike
schools, the collegiate enrollment does not have the power of
State compulsion supporting it.

It is hard to avoid the conclusion that the views of the New
York group and those in the HEW memorandum are closer to being translated into public policy than is the position of Chancellor
Caldwell. Our reason for saying this is a simple one. It is that
intelligent and serious-minded men do not invent and live by fictions unless they are thereby enabled to achieve a goal which is
very important to them. To the extent that such things are ever
fully clear, it is now clear that a compelling national interest in
higher education has been recognized and widely accepted. As a
first step this interest was made national policy by the National
Defense Education Act; as a second step it was manifest in the
activity in both the 86th and 87th Congresses for an academic
facilities building program. Without trying to predict what the third
step will be, one need not be a seer to know that it will come and
that it is likely to be broader than its predecessors.

A good clue as to a probable resolution of the issue in order
to achieve the objective was offered in the House in 1961. A special
subcommittee of the House Committee on Education and Labor,
chaired by Representative Edith Green of Oregon, developed impressive bipartisan support for the view that distinctions on religious
grounds should not be made among *institutions,* but rather among
the *activities* of each institution. H.R. 8900, therefore, treated all
institutions alike, but prohibited expenditures of Federal funds in
any institution for sectarian purposes. If there is real desire for a
Federal program of aid to colleges and universities, this approach
could neutralize the acid of the Church-State issue.[7]

There is no doubt that the broader the program is, the louder
will be the controversy over the separation of Church and State.

The point to keep in mind, for it is central to both strategy and tactics, is that, at bottom, the dispute will not be over constitutional doctrine, but over desirable social and political policy. These are legitimate grounds for debate; the arguments will be no less fierce, and they will surely be clothed in constitutional terms.

The precedents clearly chart the course ahead, however. All sides in the debate will adhere to the principle of the separation of Church and State. At the same time, there is likely to be shown a good deal of ingenuity in the application of that principle.[8]

FEDERAL CONTROL OF EDUCATION

We have made the point elsewhere that Americans have been more sophisticated than most peoples in controlling the exercise of political power by devising means of parceling it out among a number of participants. Thus, the powers of the National Government are divided among the three coordinate branches of the Federal establishment, and political power at large is formally distributed by the Constitution among the National Government, the States, and the people.

The Constitution, as adopted in 1787, of course, nowhere says explicitly that the National Government has only those powers specifically enumerated, all others being reserved for other parties. However, this was certainly the understanding of most of the delegates to the Constitutional Convention, and in particular of James Madison, its most influential member.

In the debate attending ratification of the Constitution in several State conventions, it was evident that the logic of the document itself did not satisfy everyone. So, last among the 10 amendments adopted soon after ratification was one which said, "The powers not delegated to the United States by the Constitution, nor prohibited by it to the States, are reserved to the States respectively, or to the people."

Madison himself saw no particular need for this language—

indeed, this was his feeling about some other parts of the Bill of Rights—but on the other hand, he saw no special danger in it, since it merely made explicit that which he knew was implicit in the Constitution. Good politician that he was, therefore, he welcomed the bonus of new confidence in the infant Government that this largely declaratory statement produced.

As it was proved in the event, Madison's estimate was correct, for the Tenth Amendment has had little operative significance in our constitutional history. It has not been a guide to action, and only in a limited sense has it been truly a guide to interpretation. For it has become clear over the years that the enumerated powers of the Central Government have implications far beyond their manifest content.

If there is a lesson here, it is probably the oft-told one that each generation will decide for itself just how limited or extensive it wants its government to be, and a formula of words cannot be expected to bind the hands of future generations in facing their own problems. This is not, of course, an argument for big government, small government, or any other kind of government. It is, rather, a judgment that the meaning of "a government of limited powers," or "federalism," or any other similar concept, is not decided on the basis of immutable truths, but on the basis of year-to-year—indeed, day-to-day—decisions made in political and social combat. It is in this combat, in fact, that the Tenth Amendment has its chief use, for it has served through our history as both the rallying point and battle call for those forces in the society that, for a variety of reasons, have opposed measures that make use of the powers of the Federal Government.

To put it another way, the Tenth Amendment is to conservatives what the so-called "general-welfare clause" is to liberals. They are the favorites of the pamphleteers, with the difference that the latter is part of an actual grant of power, while the former is a limitation that has not in fact markedly inhibited the exercise of Federal power.

In the periodic discussions of the Federal interest in education, the argument from the Tenth Amendment is translated into a defense of State and local control of education or, conversely, into a warning against the dangers of Federal control, which is supposed to flow inevitably from Federal participation.

The issue of Federal control is not an easy one to discuss, for it is not easy to get hold of as an entity. It means different things to different people, and is used for a variety of different purposes. It is not at all cynical, as we shall see, to say that it is often used to obscure issues that are most potent if left in obscurity. So visible is the issue, however, and so hardy a perennial is it in the consideration of Federal assistance to education that it is necessary to try to come to grips with it, to separate the appearance from the reality, and to face up to that which is real while recognizing deception where it exists.

The Issue of Control

How is the issue usually put? As good a source as any to answer this question is the National Association of Manufacturers. In its report, *Federal Expenditure Control and the 1959 Budget,* the National Association of Manufacturers said:

> In all the proposals for Federal aid heretofore advanced, vigorous disclaimers have been made to emphasize that there is no intention of exerting Federal control over curricula, school management, or other aspects of local responsibility. These assertions have always been open to challenge on the grounds, first, that "he who pays the piper calls the tune," and second, that there would be neglect of Federal responsibility in the failure to exercise supervision over the way Federal grants were used. These grounds lead to the unavoidable conclusion that there will be, and in fact must be, controls by the Federal Government to the extent that it provides funds. Obviously the more money it provides, the more control it will exercise.

This is a fair representation of the issue as it appears in public debate. The essential parts of the argument are, first, that "he who pays the piper calls the tune," and second, that the Government would be remiss if it did not seek to supervise the way in which its money was being spent. Rarely is the position extended to a point where it may be seen precisely how the piper calls the tune, that is, the mechanism through which the calling is done, or the type of supervision which does in fact accompany Federal funds. It might advance understanding if we were to examine these items in somewhat more detail.

Seduction and More

There are many ways of reaching an objective that involves inducing people to behave in a way that is different from their normal behavior. The methods range from physical coercion, through seduction, to persuasion by means of superior intellectual resources. The means may vary according to the taste, scruples, and ability of the controller, but whatever the means, the process is surely one of control.

What, however, if the same result is achieved without anyone consciously willing it? There are, certainly, many cases in which, through blundering, inadvertence, or simple human failure to foresee all consequences of an action, a wholly unintended result comes to pass. Since, taken literally, the argument *against* Federal participation in education is predicated on the assumption of the harmful results that flow from it, we must include this in our definition of control.

We have, then, several different kinds of control that range along several spectrums with regard to intention, visibility, efficacy, harmfulness of results, desirability of objectives, and no doubt others as well. The issue is a good deal more complex than at first glance it seems to be. (It is, that is, unless one subscribes to the notion that there is a conspiracy among Federal officials to dominate American education. The conspiracy theory, held by some, claims too much and explains too little, so we shall leave it to those for whom the real world is too complicated.) The subtleties have been hidden by the assumption which seems to underlie all warnings over the dangers of Federal control that there is no experience on which to base informed judgments. The fact is, as we have seen, that there is a wealth of experience in the relations between the Federal Government and higher education and that a great deal of evidence is available if anyone wants to take the trouble to use it. We shall try.

The Record

If we understand "control" to mean inducing others to do what one wants done, then it is clear that the Government has been "guilty" of this. It must be admitted that higher education would look very different today were it not for the inducements offered by the Land-Grant College Act in 1862. But this is hardly the insidious process that people refer to when expressing concern over Federal control. In that case a clear objective was stated and tangible inducements offered to any State that wanted to help in reaching that objective. Almost every Federal program in education since then has been more or less of that character.

Having admitted the existence of Federal control of this nature, we must complicate the picture by asking whether control is being exercised in cases where the effect of Government assistance is either to help States or institutions do better or more of that which they are already doing, or to help them do at all what they would like to do but cannot afford. For it must also be said that many Federal programs have been addressed to either or both of those situations. Granted, there is an element of seduction even in the latter case, since Government funds, as we have seen, are not always available for those things that institutions would like *most* to do. Under some circumstances seduction may be a crime, but it is quite a different crime from rape. This is an aspect of the nature and pattern of Federal programs that is extremely important to this discussion, and we shall return to it shortly. First, though, we should consider several more obvious types of potential control.

Control and Educational Content

A fear often expressed, and certainly implicit in the National Association of Manufacturers' statement quoted earlier, is that the Federal Government will somehow adversely influence the content of instructional programs and the point of view of both texts and instructors. There is no doubt that, if true, this is the most serious charge that could be made, and it would cast grave doubt on the justification for any Federal program of which it was true.

Fortunately, the evidence here is not at all ambiguous. As already suggested, Federal programs have had a heavy impact on the emphasis given to various parts of the curriculum. For example, there is little doubt that the heavy infusion of Federal money into the sciences has caused, or made it possible for, institutions of higher education to do things in the sciences that they would not have done in its absence. However, it is clear that there is no evidence whatsoever that Federal officials have attempted to influence the substance of any course or discipline or have done so by indirection. The distinction is a crucial one, for it goes to the very heart of the issue of Federal control. It holds, incidentally, even in cases such as the training grants programs of the National Institutes of Health, in which the Government for many years has been paying the salary of full-time faculty members. Traditions of academic freedom, indeed our whole conception of how a free society must operate, would cause all academic people to resist bitterly and effectively control of content, whatever the circumstances and whoever the attempted controller. Whatever qualms one might have about the wisdom of any given program, or about the direction of the Federal effort as a whole, can be argued as matters of educational, political, and social policy, without challenge to the integrity of higher education or the values that sustain it.

The Problem of the Mice

Another arm in the arsenal of those concerned over Federal control of education, actual or potential, is the charge that in the execution of its basic responsibility to safeguard public funds, the Government inevitably exercises a measure of control and must do so if it is to meet its obligations. Manifestly, this is true, but except by innuendo it proves little. If the statement means only that the Government must guard against misappropriation of money—that is, actual dishonesty—there can be no disagreement. If, in addition, the statement means that steps must be taken to ensure that public money is spent for the purposes intended, there must still be substantial agreement. If it means, too, that the recipient of public funds is almost certain to be burdened with time-consuming, probably expensive, and certainly annoying tasks in accounting for his use of those funds, most experienced people would have to nod agreement. Charles Kidd put this point well in his discussion of the administration of Federal research support:

> Critical observations by universities, it should be noted, relate to administrative matters rather than to the substance of research. The Federal administrators are rarely accused of attempting to influence the substance of research. I have heard of only one instance in which a Federal administrative official undertook to influence a line of investigation, and he was quickly repudiated by his superior. The complaint of university people is not that the system results in Federal control of research, but that it makes them feel as if they were being nibbled to death by mice.[9]

Actually, the problem is not a humorous one at all, for overadministration can be harassing and demoralizing. A balanced view of the situation, however, suggests that the complaints are aimed not at administration, but at *bad* administration, and that is found about as often in universities, foundations, and State and local governments as it is in the Federal Government.[10] Often in research, the Federal problem is an unwillingness or inability to distinguish between a contract for procurement and one for research. In the former certain conditions are necessary, where in the latter they may be inappropriate or harmful. The problem of the mice is not limited to the administration of research funds, but it is most noticeable there.

"The Parade of Horrors"

As it is frequently used, the term Federal control carries with it the connotation of ultimate Federal dominance of the entire educational system. Critics of Federal programs in education do not necessarily assert that any one of them of and by itself effects control, but that each may—or even, will—*lead* to Federal control. Thus Federal control is conceived as a general condition—a malaise —that represents the cumulative effect of a series of actions. In some cases concern is simply expressed in terms of how dependent upon Federal support an institution can afford to become. In other cases the clear assumption is that one Federal action having an effect on education leads inevitably to the general condition, much as one drink leads to alcoholism.

What frequently distinguishes the informed and the uninformed uses of an argument of this sort is the extent to which an assumption of inevitability is employed. It is a perfectly tenable position to be concerned about the degree of institutional dependence upon any single source of support, including the Federal Government, just as it is considered wise to diversify an investment portfolio or to "hedge" racetrack bets. Thus, for example, did the "Heald Commission" in New York State recommend a bold program of State aid to private institutions, but enter the following advice:

> Although the direct aid we propose is for the purpose of strengthening private institutions and permitting private higher education to continue as a substantial and influential factor in New York State, the payments should not be so large as to change the character of private institutions—particularly so as

to make them too heavily dependent on the State for their future financing. We believe that an aggregate payment not in excess of 10 per cent of teaching expenditures in private colleges and universities in the State would satisfy these requirements.

A less responsible use of the argument seems to suggest that no limits can be placed upon a Federal-institutional relationship once begun; that a first kiss leads inexorably to the total surrender of virtue. A terribly Victorian view, to say the least. In the view of those who take this position and make this use of the Federal-control issue, institutions are helpless to resist the encroachments of government. The autonomy of higher education is threatened by "creeping" Federal aid and "insidious" Federal envelopment. The lurid manner in which the inevitability of all this is described has led to its being dubbed the "parade of horrors" argument. The users of this argument are notoriously unconcerned about "alumni control" or "state control" or "faculty control" of higher education and impart a particularly evil and voracious quality to the Federal Government.

There is at least one university president whose experience with the Federal Government sheds a different light on this subject. Chancellor Jaime Benitez, for more than twenty years head of the University of Puerto Rico, made this observation in 1961:

> I am for federal aid to education on two basic considerations. I think (*a*) here is where there is most money with least controls. We oftentimes talk about federal influence and federal control of monies that are received, and I just would invite my colleagues who have been getting monies throughout the years to consider the correlation of pressures to amounts of monies obtained, and inquire from them: where do the most pressures come for oftentimes the least monies you get?
>
> I would say the amount of pressures proportionate to the amount of money that comes from the Federal government is insignificant if you measure them against the amount of pres-

sures you would get for lesser amounts of money from private donors, from the state, and from foundations.[11]

The plain fact of the matter is that autonomy and freedom and independence in higher education, as in all walks of life, are largely matters of spirit rather than substance. In so far as material factors play a part in kindling or extinguishing this spirit—in so far as it *is* true that he who pays the piper calls the tune—much can in fact be said *in favor* of Federal assistance to higher education. Unless one can bring himself to attribute essential evil to the Federal Government—which the authors confess they cannot—there appear to be positive benefits (in terms of true institutional autonomy) in a broad base of financial support. A workable twentieth-century definition of institutional autonomy would be the absence of dependence upon a single or narrow base of financial support. There is ample reason to believe that the availability of Federal funds can relieve institutions from too great dependence upon domineering or disdainful patrons and thus permit freer expression of institutional values.

Oaths, Affidavits, and the Loyalty-Security Complex

The passage of the National Defense Education Act brought to public attention what many educators believe to be the most serious overt threat which the Government poses to the integrity of higher education. This is the requirement that students receiving benefits under the National Defense Education Act swear an oath of loyalty to the United States and disclaim membership or belief in subversive organizations. Seldom has an action of the Federal Government raised such widespread and intense resentment in the educational community. As a result, there have been two sharp debates in the Senate over elimination or amendment of the offending requirement and the withdrawal of some of the Nation's leading colleges and universities from participation in some programs of the Act. Also, some difficult moral decisions involving other Federal programs with similar requirements had to be made by institutions of higher education, and were frequently made on what seemed to be narrow and even ambiguous grounds.

In broad terms, the controversy over the oath and affidavit is a part of the larger issue of loyalty and security requirements as they apply to educational efforts that came to a head in the area of sponsored research in the early 1950s. The National Defense Education Act has received more publicity largely because it has been handled in the legislative arena rather than in the relatively more quiet administrative processes, as was the case with research. Seeing the problem whole, though, there is little doubt that the research problem posed a far more direct and serious challenge to educational processes than the National Defense Education Act oath and affidavit. It will be instructive, then, to look briefly at the former, for if there is, inherent in Federal programs, the imminent threat of requirements offensive to basic principles of academic freedom, then there is indeed reason to question the wisdom of Federal participation in higher education.

There is little question that some safeguards are required when military secrecy is involved, and a few institutions have declined to accept classified research out of a conviction that secrecy is inappropriate to the academic atmosphere. It is the application of these safeguards to nonsecret work—health research, for example—that has caused the problem. The greatest abuses occurred at the height of the McCarthy era, and the resolution of the problem was virtually coterminous with the decline of the Senator from Wisconsin.

No sober person can look back on that period without a sense of shame over the personal damage done to so many people in pursuit of an illusory concept of national security. It does not end with the harm done to individuals, however, for the threat to the institutions of a free society and to the very values that nourish freedom itself was of a magnitude seldom equaled in our history. There are two things to be said, however, neither of which excuse the fear and hysteria which gripped the Federal Government but both of which are important to an understanding of the whole problem. First, as bad as were the acts of the Federal Government, its shame must be shared by virtually every part of the society. Parts of the business community, the churches, and higher education itself were all too willing to sacrifice inconvenient principles for temporary comfort. In short, the malaise of the 1950s was a national rather than a governmental affliction. And second, it ended. Balance was restored, and our central values emerged, if not triumphant, at least still alive and vital.

There is no doubt that the academic community emerged from the McCarthy era shaken and with at least a measure of self-guilt. Undoubtedly, this has accounted in part for the severe reaction to the oath and affidavit provisions of the National Defense Education Act when similar provisions have been in force in National Science Foundation and National Institutes of Health programs for many years. There is also no doubt that, if balance has been restored, it is by definition not a fixed, but rather a changing, one, for it is the result of pressures and counterpressures. The events of the McCarthy era were not inevitable, nor is their recurrence. This does not in any way deny or underestimate the danger of potential threats to freedom in education and in other areas, as well. Rather, it asserts that we do not live in a Greek tragedy, and the position of the stars does not govern human events. To the contrary, we live in a society which provides ample opportunity for any group which thinks itself aggrieved to bring to bear whatever lawful force it is able to command in defense of its interests.

The heated controversy over the disclaimer affidavit in the National Defense Education Act is an excellent example of the way in which the normal political processes provide both a defense against offensive Government actions and a means for reaching an agreement on solutions that are generally satisfactory to the contenders to a dispute.

In 1959, a group of Senators, led by the then Senator Kennedy, attempted to strike from the NDEA both the affirmative oath of allegiance to the Constitution and the negative disclaimer affidavit. This attempt failed, and in the course of the debate on it, it became clear that a majority could not be mobilized to eliminate the former, but that progress could be made if future efforts were concentrated on the much more offensive disclaimer affidavit. Thus, in 1960 the Senate debated the narrower but more important issue of the affidavit. It again became clear that a majority of the Senate would not subscribe to simply eliminating the provision and that a way would have to be found to deny benefits of the Act to members of subversive groups. The Senate finally passed an amendment proposed by Senator Winston Prouty of Vermont, which made it a crime for an individual who knowingly belonged to a "subversive" organization to accept benefits under the Act, but freed participating institutions from any direct involvement in the relationship. In 1961, the Senate Committee on Labor and Public Welfare arrived at an even more precise requirement. The Committee proposed that it be made a crime for any member of an organization, required to register as a communist organization by a final order of the Subversive Activities Control Board, to apply for NDEA benefits.

Thus, the issue was narrowed by these two actions to that of finding the best means of denying benefits to members of subversive groups without requiring a general disclaimer of disloyalty by all applicants—an issue that would appear capable of resolution without offense to the integrity of institutions of higher education. The approach devised by the Senate Committee appeared to be an acceptable one to most educational spokesmen, but failed of adoption when other factors combined to preclude 1961 amendments to the NDEA. The approach was adopted, however, as a substitute for the disclaimer required of National Science Foundation fellows.

It would be a great mistake to draw from the various clashes over loyalty and security the conclusion that Federal funds must always be accompanied by repugnant conditions. The evidence leads rather to the conclusion that there is vitality enough in our political system to ensure against the imposition of such conditions on those who are vigilant in defense of their freedoms and to offer recourse for their repair when such excesses do occur.

The Short Run and the Long Run

If the threat of an unwelcome intrusion upon educational matters must be guarded against, there is another kind of threat which is less obvious but perhaps even more imminent. It is the danger that comes from too much extemporizing; from too great a reliance on stopgaps and crash programs; and in general from too high a regard for immediately visible needs and measurable results and too little concern for the long-term health of the educational system. One observer has put it this way:

> . . . No evidence has been found for the existence of direct controls by the Federal Government, or any of its agencies, over either public or private higher education or for the desire for such controls. What does exist is an influence over the program and policies of higher education resulting from the many separate, uncoordinated federal programs in higher education, each of which emphasizes the interests of the federal department or agency sponsoring it rather than the general needs of higher education.[12]

This is a problem of indirection rather than direction; of lack of control rather than control. It does not, it should be added, result from the Government's doing things it should not be doing. Virtually every Federal program currently operating in the area of higher education can be justified as meeting some national need that would not be met in its absence. As we have seen, however, these are needs that are essentially noneducational, but in the fulfillment of which educational institutions are indispensable.

Obviously, the dichotomy is not as sharp as we make it sound, but the sharp separation is necessary in order to make it clear that only rarely have responsible Government policy makers been in a position to view the needs of higher education, in its own right, or failing that, at least to view the possible distorting effects of the variety of present programs. The latter is especially important, for it is probably unrealistic to expect the Government ever to have a comprehensive and systematic approach to higher education. If it is, then it becomes all the more important to consider carefully the potential distortion—control, if you will—that results from programs which are largely scientific, largely affecting graduate education, and largely limited to a few universities.

This is a kind of control which does not get much public attention, for it does not carry with it the kinds of overt interference or covert insinuation that are usually thought to constitute Federal control. In addition, attention to this problem presupposes a concern for education and a commitment to the wisdom or necessity of appropriate Federal assistance that are not usually found among those who express the greatest concern over what they see as the inevitability of Federal control. Indeed, the opposition of such people to proposals that might shape Federal programs into a balanced whole has had the effect of bringing closer the day when the damage to higher education from an excess of *ad hoc* activity will be irretrievable.

But we do not think that the responsibility for avoiding distortion of this kind rests with the Government alone. There are two parties to the arrangement, and the "taker" shares responsibility with the "giver." This view was put well, recently, in a personal letter to the authors:

> It has seemed to me . . . that the strength of purpose, the intellectual vigor, and the unity of purpose of an institution are strong bulwarks against Federal control. The Federal agencies and Federal money will tend to set policy for an institution more or less in direct proportion to the absence of a strong policy by the institution itself. In many respects undesirable consequences assumed to flow from Federal aid actually flow from the intellectual flabbiness of the schools in dealing with Federal funds. It takes some experience, I suppose, to use money effectively when the absence of money has been such a

convenient excuse for the absence of policy on many issues. One of the challenges of Federal aid to education would, in my judgment, be the challenge to the universities to use Federal funds productively and in accordance with stated university policies. If the precedent in research is any guide, I suspect that many schools would follow the lead of Federal agencies not because the Federal agencies "control" them, but because the schools have no clear policy of their own. The policies of the Federal agencies—and they must have some policies—can appear as Federal control simply because they are a substitute for nonexistent institutional policies.

In summary, I think the schools can accept Federal funds and remain free in large part in proportion to the degree to which they have a sound and consistent philosophy and translate this philosophy into actual operating decisions.

The Real and the Unreal

We said earlier in this discussion that the issue of Federal control is one in which it is most difficult to separate the appearance from the reality, because it is used not only as a genuine argument against Federal assistance, but also as a guise to hide other motives. Chief among the other factors that lie behind the argument over Federal control are the pocketbook, as represented by tax policy, and the segregation issue.

As with so many other features of Federal educational policy, the issues here are seen most clearly in discussions of Federal aid to elementary and secondary education. Debate over the abortive school-aid bill of 1960 provided an instructive example of the peculiar mixture which is so characteristic of arguments about Federal control. The particular point that interests us was an amendment to the bill offered by Representative Phillip M. Landrum of Georgia. The amendment read:

> Notwithstanding any provision of this act, or of any other law, or of any rule, regulation, decision, or action made or taken under this act or under such other law, the laws or prac-

tices of a State, or of a political subdivision of a State, with respect to the personnel, program of instruction, formulation of policy, and the administration and operation of the public elementary and secondary schools in the State shall in no way disqualify such State for any grant under this act or affect in any manner the amount of such grant, and no such provision shall be deemed to require or permit the imposition of any requirement, condition, or restriction on, or in any way control or affect the uses which may be made of such funds when granted to the State, because of the laws or practices of the State or of a political subdivision thereof with respect to the personnel, program of instruction, formulation of policy, or the administration and operation of the public elementary and secondary schools in the State.

The purpose of the Landrum amendment is evident from the reference in the opening sentence to "any other law, or of any rule, regulation, decision, or action." It is neither more nor less than an attempt to prevent the administrators of the law from denying funds to a State or school district that practices segregation of the races. It is a "Powell amendment" in reverse. An amendment using the bald terms which we have used to describe it, however, would be wholly unacceptable to the natural allies of its sponsor, namely, those who oppose Federal aid on still other grounds but will use any position which is on its face politically respectable. One such ally, a Representative from a Midwestern State, made the following comments, in which he linked the Landrum amendment to still another amendment proposed by Representative Frank T. Bow of Ohio:

> As was to be expected, we heard a considerable amount of discussion concerning the Federal control contained in this bill. The Chairman of the House Education and Labor Committee, the Honorable Graham A. Barden of North Carolina, opposed the bill and stated, "I know there is control in the bill." However, they would not accept an amendment offered by the

Honorable Phil M. Landrum of Georgia, which would have written a provision into the law against Federal control. The Landrum amendment would have provided the necessary insurance against Federal Control. . . .

Had the proponents of this legislation meant what they said when they stated that there was no Federal control in this bill they would have agreed to the inclusion of this amendment in the law.[13]

At this point in his remarks the speaker demonstrated how gracefully the Federal-control specter can be allied with conservative tax policy:

Apparently the sponsors of this legislation wanted more than Federal money for education, otherwise, they would not have rejected the proposal of the Honorable Frank T. Bow, of Ohio. The Federal Government levies a tax of 8 cents on each package of cigarettes sold within our borders. Under Cong. Bow's proposal, the Secretary of the Treasury would have been authorized to return to each State 2 cents of the 8 cents collected by the Federal Government in that State.

The frequency with which opposition to Federal educational assistance based on the danger of Federal control is linked to tax-reform schemes suggests that there is something more than a chance relationship. Most commonly, such proposals contemplate a refund to the States of a portion of some Federal tax. The soundness of this device on its merits is open to serious question, and it has in fact consistently been opposed by the executive branch, whichever political party has been in office.[14] Apart from being bad tax policy and a haphazard way of distributing tax potential between the Federal Government and the States, it is bad educational policy, and poor public policy in general, in that it bases the support to education on sales of a wholly unrelated set of goods or services and provides no chance for even the roughest kind of equalization among the richer and poorer States. If the tax rebate is earmarked for education, it shares all the commonly recognized disabilities of earmarked revenues, and if it is not, there is no guarantee at all that the money would be used for educational purposes.

Regardless of the merits of any particular scheme of tax reform, however, the underlying point is that those who prescribe them as preventive medicine against Federal control usually are diagnosing for noneducational ills. The drive, prevalent among economic conservatives, to turn—or return, depending on one's point of view—Federal tax sources over to the States goes far beyond the area of education. It is, indeed, part of a much larger view of the proper scope of Government activity, of which the fear of Federal control over education, however sincerely felt, is but a part.

We have already noted that the confusion of appearance with reality, so much a part of the processes of politics, becomes harmful when it prevents full and open discussion of genuine issues. If advocates of a particular objective have a right to try to reach that objective by masking it behind another—and they do—then their opponents have an equal right to try to take the mask from the face. The debate over Federal control has suffered from a failure at unmasking.

Last Words from History

Perhaps the last word on the issue of Federal control was written before the issue was ever known to exist. Alexander Hamilton said it: "In framing a government which is to be administered by men over men, the great difficulty lies in this: you must first enable the government to control the governed, and in the next place oblige it to control itself." Evidence has yet to be brought forward that, in the area of education, the two are out of balance.

SEGREGATION

As we have suggested, the issues under discussion here vary in their degree of visibility as well as in their essential importance. It must be clear that the authors regard the issue of Federal control as having a degree of substance greatly exaggerated by its degree of visibility. The so-called Church-State issue is somewhat the reverse; while not frequently brought out into the open, it is present in the minds of many who play an active role in relationships between the Federal Government and higher education. Indeed, the authors believe that the failure to discuss the so-called Church-State issue openly and fully has tended to perpetuate cloudy misconceptions.

The so-called segregation issue resembles more the Church-State issue than it does that of Federal control, in the sense that it receives relatively little public attention (as for example in the halls of the Congress) even though it lies at the root of much stubborn opposition to Federal programs in education. It is reasonable to assume that fuller and more candid discussion of this issue could, as in the case of the Church-State issue, bring about a lessening of submerged hostilities and thus permit progress toward more constructive policies. It must be counted as a truth in public affairs that the potency of some issues is heightened by the fact that they are permitted to remain under the surface of public discussion.

The basic issue is, of course, whether or not Federal funds should be spent in institutions of higher education that deny admission to qualified candidates on account of their race. There are those who believe that expenditures for the promotion of education should not be used as instruments for effecting basic social change in the South, and there are those who contend that any public expenditure in a segregated institution has the effect, not simply of perpetuating, but of reinforcing, an undesirable *status quo*. Educational programs and expenditures, linked as they are to the development of future social attitudes, are perhaps the hottest crucible in which the whole subject of race relations is being tested. Equal protection of the laws and equality of opportunity in their many other dimensions do not arouse nearly so much emotion as they do in the area of education.

Part of the difficulty of confronting higher education as it comes to grips with this issue is that it suffers from its association with the problem as expressed in the public elementary and secondary schools. Certainly something is gained from distinguishing between two quite different patterns of adjustment to racial segregation within the total structure of education.

The legal considerations, as well as the facts of segregation at the higher-education level, differ significantly from those at the level of elementary and secondary public schools. Some of these may in turn appropriately affect the public conscience as it deals with the subject:

1. Desegregation has been effected more rapidly in higher education than it has in elementary and secondary education. Consider the situation in the 17 States which have, historically, practiced racial segregation. As of late 1961, 270 public and private institutions of higher education were desegregated, either in practice or in principle. These represented about 55 per cent of the public institutions in those States and almost a third of the private institutions. In only two States (Mississippi and South Carolina) had nothing been done toward desegregation of public colleges and universities,[15] but in every one of the 17 Southern and Border States, at least one private college had been desegregated. Though a significant number of institutions still deny admission to Negroes, these institutions enroll a minority of students in the South. Desegregated institutions, as of 1961, enrolled 62.75 per cent of all students in institutions of these 17 States. It would appear that there is less resistance, or at least less effective resistance, among Southern citizens to the desegregation of institutions of higher education than there is to the desegregation of lower schools. By the same token, those who seek to effect racial desegregation in the South may find less to be impatient about in the higher-education picture.

2. Public colleges and universities look to a distinctive set of Federal court decisions for illumination of the legal aspects of segregation. Whereas the constitutionality of public school practices

is to be measured against the 1954 decisions of the Supreme Court, higher education looks to a series of cases culminating in the *Sweat v. Painter* decision of 1950, involving the admission of a Negro to the University of Texas Law School. While in the Texas Law School case the court did not consider directly the question of the validity of the "separate but equal" tradition, it did make clear that certain factors such as tradition, prestige, and the opportunity to associate in school with members of the dominant group make it practically impossible to provide truly equal facilities when they are separate.[16] The most dramatic difference between the 1950 decision affecting public higher education and the 1954 decisions affecting public elementary and secondary education is the fact that the Supreme Court made no provision for "gradualism" in the case of the University of Texas. Nor has the court in a series of subsequent decisions affecting public institutions of higher education used any such term as "deliberate speed." In every instance, the Court has ordered the immediate admission of qualified persons denied admission on grounds of race.

3. Supreme Court decisions have a vastly more far-reaching social effect when applied to the public schools than when applied to public colleges and universities. The vast majority of all children in the South are enrolled in public schools, largely as a result of compulsory school attendance laws and because there is no significant tradition of nonpublic schools. On both counts, the situation in higher education is significantly different. As in the rest of the Nation, only a minority of the college-age population is enrolled in college and there is a strong tradition of a private alternative to public higher education. In this sense, the South as a society may feel less affected by desegregation at the collegiate level than it is by general educational desegregation.

4. The great majority of present Federal expenditures in institutions of higher education do not appear to constitute support of institutions, segregated or desegregated, so much as they do the utilization of specific resources within the institutions. The fact

that the Federal Government seems to be reaching *into* rather than *to* an institution makes a difference to many persons. It is of interest to note, for example, that Representative Adam Clayton Powell of New York, in 1958, considered that it would be "inappropriate" for him to attach his famed antisegregation amendment to the National Defense Education Act. Contract expenditures for the purchase of services, however much they may strengthen institutions, do not touch directly on the sensitive matters of admission and social practice.

Given these distinctive characteristics of the pattern of relationships in higher education, it is not surprising to note that Federal funds do flow to segregated colleges and universities. Nonetheless, there are those who would deny or withhold Federal funds from such institutions, either through legislative requirement or administrative action. Herein lies what may emerge as the really root cause of trouble in the whole issue: Who is to determine the public policy and how?

Denying funds to segregated institutions through the legislative mechanism is one thing; withholding funds through executive action is quite another. For reasons that are widely known, Southern spokesmen would much prefer that the issue be resolved or at least contained legislatively. Essentially, they recognize that given our Federal system of representation and the unique character of our legislative structure, their voice is greater in this branch of Government than it is ever likely to be in the executive or judicial branches. But apart from this realistic and hardheaded basis for their views, Southern legislators also point to the Fourteenth Amendment and to the Constitution itself. They assert that the Amendment guaranteeing equal protection of the laws is not self-enforcing. Their case rests in the final clause of that Amendment: "The Congress shall have power to enforce this article by appropriate legislation."

Whether or not, as Southern legislators contend, it is the exclusive responsibility of the Congress to implement the equal-protection guarantee of the Constitution, it is worth examining the temper and attitude of Congress on this issue. A few historical evidences may clarify the attitudes of the legislative branch of Government, however little light they may shed on the constitutional issues involved. In its only legislative action clearly touching on the issue of segregation in higher education—the Second Morrill Act—the Congress condoned the practice of separate institutions for Negroes and whites. The 1890 Act said in part: ". . . The establishment and maintenance of such colleges separately for white and colored students shall be held to be in compliance with the provisions of this Act if the funds received in such State or Territory be equitably divided. . . ." Through subsequent amendments to this Act and appropriations thereunder, the Congress has not, apparently, altered its position. The action to amend the Act in 1960 is especially striking, since it took place after the Supreme Court had clearly abandoned its former position on the separate-but-equal concept.

Because it is the only major new piece of educational legislation enacted since the pertinent Supreme Court decisions, the National Defense Education Act affords an especially interesting insight into Congressional attitudes, though the Act makes no reference to segregation as such. In the first instance, the Act states:

> Sec. 102. Nothing contained in this Act shall be construed to authorize any department, agency, officer, or employee of the United States to exercise any direction, supervision, or control over the curriculum, program of instruction, administration, or personnel of any educational institution or school system.

Even more interesting, however, is the following even more specific language, which was a part of the legislation as it was adopted by the Senate, and as it went to conference:

> Part D. Sec. 531. The eligibility of applicants for admission to institutes under the provisions of this title shall be determined by the institutions of higher education operating such institutes.

Those concerned with the subject of Congressional intent may well wonder why it is that this highly specific language failed to appear in the Act as finally adopted by the Congress and signed by the President. It may serve not only to clarify the legislative history of this Act, but as well to shed light on the legislative process, to report that the language appears in fact to have been approved by conferees representing both House and Senate, and to report further the legend that it would have been included in the final bill had it not been for the opinion of Congressional staff members who regarded it as unnecessary in view of Section 102, quoted above. So hectic were the conditions surrounding the final passage of the National Defense Education Act (it was adopted on the last day of the 86th Congress) that it is quite probable that the absence of this very explicit indication of Congressional intent was overlooked in the rush.[17]

A further, and perhaps convincing, clue to Congressional attitudes is to be found in the fact that those who oppose Federal assistance to education frequently support antisegregation riders. So confident are they of Congressional sentiment on this issue that they believe such a rider will "kill" the legislation to which it is appended. This is a further indication of the intermingling of issues in opposition to Federal programs in education and another illustration of the importance of distinguishing the real and unreal foundations of opposition. But in this instance the use of desegregation threats as an effective means of forestalling legislation offers evidence both of the reality of the segregation issue and of the Congress' desire to avoid it.

This, then, is some of the evidence in support of the view that the inclination of the Congress has been—at least in the past—not to use educational programs as an instrument in effecting desegregation. Even so-called liberal legislators can and do subscribe to the position, looking sometimes to the words of Senator Hubert Humphrey of Minnesota, who, in opposing a desegregation rider in 1948, declared, "As much as I despise segregation, I love education more."

In view of the long history of legislation affecting education, these few evidences seem scant. They are hardly sufficient to justify the view that the Congress as a body approves of or condones segregation. But what is more important, perhaps, they make a fairly convincing case for the fact that the Congress does not want to have to treat the issue any more frequently or directly than is necessary.

Given this insight into the attitude of the Congress, there are those who do argue that the executive branch of the Government has it within its power to withhold funds under at least some existing legislation from institutions that deny admission to Negroes, and should do so.[18] These persons argue that in the light of Supreme Court decisions, the moral wrong of segregation is sufficiently great to warrant executive action without prior action by the Congress— a view calculated to arouse hostility among a considerable number of Congressmen, North and South. One basis for this position was presented in 1956 by then Representative Lee Metcalf of Montana, who, somewhat ironically, was arguing against the attachment of the Powell amendment to a school-construction bill. His view was that the amendment was unnecessary, since the executive branch already had sufficient authority to carry out its essentials.

> For me, too, there is a principle here that is fundamental in constitutional doctrine, that goes back to the separation of powers. I shall never concede that the enforcement of the great provisions of the Constitution, the liberties guaranteed in the Bill of Rights, and the 14th amendment are not effective until there is a specific legislative enactment by the Congress. The legislative branch of Government cannot by refusal or failure to act, deprive citizens of rights and privileges guaranteed by the Constitution. It is the duty of the executive branch to enforce these provisions of the Constitution in every law. These self-executing provisions of the Constitution are implicit in every law en-

acted by Congress and it is unnecessary to specially mention
them in legislation affecting the subjects in which these constitutional principles are involved. Without further congressional action it becomes the duty of the Commissioner of Education, the Secretary of Health, Education, and Welfare, and the
Attorney General of the United States to enforce the equal protection and due process clauses of the Constitution as soon as
clarified by the United States Supreme Court.[19]

The Civil Rights Commission, in a report made public in January, 1961, similarly urged action to withhold funds from segregated
public [20] colleges and universities, saying:

> The Supreme Court has held that the Federal Government is
> prohibited by the Constitution from maintaining racially segre-
> gated educational institutions. It is not sound policy for the
> Federal Government to subsidize the unconstitutional operations
> of others; to do indirectly what it is not permitted to do directly.
>
> It is not a sound policy for the Federal Government to dis-
> burse public funds in such a manner that it increases the adverse
> effects on some citizens of denials of equal protection of the laws
> by states and political subdivisions thereof.

Why then has not the executive branch exercised its alleged
authority?

Realistically, the reasons for the failure of the executive branch
of Government to exercise whatever authority it may have lie in
an area of judgment that involves educational and political, as well
as legal and moral, values. There is every reason to believe that
officials of the executive branch of Government are familiar with
the legal considerations involved, and there is just as good reason
to believe that they are aware of the moral overtones of this situation. With access to legal theories and propositions that would
support either position—to withhold or not to withhold—the executive branch appears to have allowed other considerations to tip the
scales of judgment.

Essentially, the educational considerations are these: In the first instance, a general policy of withholding funds from segregated institutions—either individually or, more likely, by States—would in one sense most hurt those it was intended to help. The withholding of land-grant funds from the State of Mississippi, for example, would cut off less than half of one per cent of the annual income of the all-white university and some 6 per cent of the income of the separate Negro institution. But more importantly, a withholding policy that disregarded the tenderness of the Congress on this issue would inspire at least some Congressional retaliation. However much authority the executive branch may have to withhold funds from segregated institutions, it is still dependent upon Congress to appropriate funds for its educational programs. In the absence of any clear Congressional desire to initiate desegregation efforts, the Congress might refuse to support financially Federal programs that were used for this purpose.[21] The result might well be no appropriations for existing educational programs. The net effect, therefore, while constituting a social gain in the minds of most Americans, would have to be regarded as an educational setback.

Strictly political considerations seem also to suggest the conclusion that, realistically speaking, the executive branch cannot by itself resolve the issue, because in one form or another, e.g., appropriations, it will find its way into the Congress, ultimately to be resolved there. There are two basically conflicting views of this issue, however. It is either an educational issue, with other considerations, moral and ideological, secondary, or it is an overriding issue of civil rights which happens to involve education.[22] For those who take the former view, the strategy is to avoid in every way possible introducing segregation as a legislative or executive consideration. For those who take the latter view, it is expedient to argue that *only* the executive can force resolution of the issue, because the Congress, given its power structure, will always find ways to avoid it.

Assuming that the full power and prestige of the Presidency were to be thrown into an effort to effect desegregation of higher education as a part of larger public policy, grave political considerations would have to be taken into account. If Congressional sentiment is in fact—as the record would seem to indicate—opposed to stirring up the issue, it is no exaggeration to say that any President would be risking his entire legislative program—to say nothing of the political future of himself and his party—to act unilaterally. A hostile Congress can, as history makes clear, blunt or even break the sharpest of executive lances. It would be folly, therefore, to disregard the extensive political ramifications of an executive action taken without at least some semblance of Congressional concurrence.

In all probability, it is a set of realistic factors built around these educational and political considerations that will determine Federal policy on the desegregation issue in higher education. So long as the Congress, in terms of essential power and of attitude, remains constant, so in all likelihood will public policy on this issue. Independent viewers of the issue may lean strongly to a more clear-cut resolution, but the facts seem to indicate that the subtle and elusive forces at play within the Congress will in the last analysis forge the public policy.

The Resolution of Divisive Issues

The three major issues of public policy discussed here—relations between Church and State, Federal control of education, and segregation—are not limited to education alone. All three, including the broad issue of the expansion of Federal power, of which the issue of Federal control is but one aspect, cut across the political system and touch a variety of other specific policy areas. They are, in a sense, overarching issues, and they all can be traced back to bitter conflicts somewhere in our history.

To many people each is a dominant issue, so important in their scale of values that maintaining and asserting the "right" position takes priority over any other consideration.

The genius of American politics, though, lies in the ability to avoid irreconcilable conflicts by making adjustments that allow all but the most bitter partisans consolation for their beliefs. So important is this process of political adjustment that its one complete failure in the 1850s led to a conflict whose effects are still evident.

In addition to the "true believers," all important issues attract people who are not so much dedicated to a position as they are ready to use a position for other ends. These "issue users," too, are an important part of the complex set of forces in motion in the process of framing public policy. It should be noted that the motives of the "issue users" are not necessarily mean or base, nor are their tactics considered outside the bounds of political fair play. The three issues we have discussed are each, from time to time, used by people for whom they are not controlling issues, in order to reach an objective considered by them to be important. Perhaps the most graphic example of this is the now familiar sight of conservative Northern Congressmen voting for antisegregation amendments to education bills in the knowledge that the adoption of such an amendment would secure defeat of the entire bill. Each one of our triumvirate lends itself to similar, if not quite so dramatic, uses.

Higher education, as we have seen, has managed to avoid overt legislative conflict over these issues for a special set of reasons. Broadly speaking, these reasons are embraced under the proposition that the products of higher education have been seen to be so important to some critical national effort that skillful legislators have devised ways of circumventing trouble. This, combined with extreme sensitivity to these issues by administrative officials, has resulted in a relatively placid surface.

Lost in the process, however, has been the kind of Government activity that most educators believe to be most needed, namely, general assistance to institutions to strengthen them in the exercise of all their functions as institutions of higher education. We have suggested that the closer a government program comes to that goal, the more likely it is to come within the range of one or more of the major issues; to come within range, that is, of the very forces which most threaten its defeat.

It is fair to say, we believe, that proposals bearing on higher education will in the future be subject to two drives. The first is the political tendency to avoid thorny issues wherever possible. The second is the drive—resulting from an increasing public awareness of the importance of higher education—toward broader programs aimed at buttressing the structure of higher education. The result, if recent history is a trustworthy guide, is liable to be twofold; we are likely, first, to see growing contention over the application of Church-State relations, Federal control, and segregation to higher education. We are likely to see also, however, further small steps toward broader and broader programs of Federal action. It is in conflicts such as these that the mettle of a political system is tested.

NOTES

[1] 330 U.S. 1 (1947).

[2] 343 U.S. 306 (1952).

[3] *Proceedings of the 72nd Annual Convention of the American Association of Land-Grant Colleges and State Universities* (Washington, D.C., 1958), pp. 312–313.

It is interesting to note a certain lack of precision in the application of terms here and elsewhere in the Church-State debate. To the best of our knowledge, no one has ever charged that aid to a nonsectarian private institution would violate the First Amendment, yet a common view seems to be that all private institutions should be excluded from public support because some are church-related. A similar "lumping" of private institutions was evident in the 1961 proposals of Senator Morse, to provide grants to public colleges and loans to private colleges, for the purchase of teaching equipment. Such gross categorization, with reverse effect, can be observed in the HEW memorandum on constitutionality, where the public need for private higher education is employed by inference in support of public aid for church-related colleges.

[4] *Meeting the Increasing Demand for Higher Education in New York State* (Albany, 1960), p. 24.

From time to time, the proposal is made that Federal funds should be channeled through the States, with each State deciding in accord with its own constitution whether the benefits should then be distributed to private and church-related institutions. The device appeals to some people because it seems to be a way of avoiding contention over the First Amendment question at the national level.

For two reasons, we believe this to be an illusion, and not a happy one at that. First, this arrangement would defer even further the development of a clear conception of what the Federal interest in higher education is. If, as we believe, that interest is to be found in appropriate action toward the strengthening of all the Nation's higher educational resources, then its realization cannot be left exclusively to the varying practices of 50 separate States.

Second, there is no reason to believe that such a device would avoid the First Amendment problem. If Federal assistance to church-related schools is truly a constitutional question, the issue would no doubt be the same whether the money were to be given directly to institutions or passed through the hands of a middleman.

There are important functions for the States in the administration of Federal programs. It would be most unwise to throw this issue to them, thereby forcing them to resolve individually what is truly a national issue.

[5] *Ibid.*, p. 24.

[6] *Ibid.*, p. 25.

[7] The American Civil Liberties Union appears to have made a similar distinction. Its 1961 witness before the Senate Subcommittee on Education testified that "Church institutions are engaged in a number of other activities beside religious activities. The problem is to discover the nature of the activity rather than the nature of the sponsorship."

[8] David D. Henry, President of the University of Illinois ["The Role of the Federal Government in Higher Education," *The Education Record* (July, 1959), pp. 202–203], has put in direct terms the "action" position on this issue: "There are those who accept the propriety of and need for federal grants to private non-church-related institutions but who question the constitutionality of a plan to include sectarian institutions. They point out that support of federal grants for church-related hospitals and church-related medical schools (for research facilities) was based upon the rationalization—insofar as this issue is involved—that the services of hospitals and research laboratories of

religious institutions are functions unrelated to religious purposes. This rationalization says that instruction even in medical schools and hospitals serves religious purposes whereas research and bedside service do not. In my view, this is a quibble.

"In any event, the issue is too important to be resolved on what congressmen and others *think* is unconstitutional. Even constitutional lawyers are divided on the point. We shall not *know* the answer until a plan is adopted and tested in the courts. . . .

"Fear of unconstitutionality, as long as informed legal opinion is divided, should not be used as a barrier to action on a plan carefully designed to minimize the risk of challenge on the religious issue."

One of the proposals given some attention in the 1961 debate on school-aid legislation was that a bill be passed providing money for private schools and that the bill include a "test clause" which would enable a challenge to its constitutionality to be taken directly to the Supreme Court for prompt decision.

[9] Charles V. Kidd, *American Universities and Federal Research* (Cambridge, Mass., 1959), p. 170.

[10] For some institutions bad Federal administration may be a more serious problem than its State, local, and private counterpart. The difference is largely one of access to the administrators and partly of psychological orientation. The Federal Government *is* large and, in some of its actions, most forbidding. There is a feeling that it is less "manageable," less "open," and consequently less prone to redress grievances against it. The evidence of institutions with extensive experience in dealing with the Federal Government suggests that, in time, the Government comes to look a good deal less awesome.

[11] *Transactions and Proceedings of the National Association of State Universities,* Vol. LVIV (sic).

[12] Richard G. Axt, *The Federal Government and Financing Higher Education* (New York, 1952), pp. 14–15.

[13] Apart from considerations of political cunning, it is probable that the claim made on behalf of the protective value of the Landrum amendment is excessive, for it is at least questionable whether any such general incantation can remove from an administrator the responsibility to carry out specific provisions of a law. But it should be noted that this consideration does not seem to lessen our faith in the magic power of words. Presumably, enough members of Congress shared that faith to include in the National Defense Education Act the statement that "Nothing contained in this Act shall be construed to authorize any

department, agency, officer, or employee of the United States to exercise any direction, supervision, or control over the curriculum, program of instruction, administration, or personnel of any educational institution or school system." Such a provision helps to set an atmosphere of administration which is desirable in achieving its end, but it is no substitute for careful draftsmanship in the substance of the law or for administrators with sensitivity of the Government's proper role in education.

[14] An exception to this was the proposal of the Eisenhower Administration to return to the States a portion of the Federal telephone tax as the *quid* for the *quo* of having the States assume financial responsibility for vocational education programs. The offer received no substantial support either in the Congress or the State houses. When the money is on the line, the indispensable partner of States' rights, namely, States' responsibility, looks less and less attractive.

We do not, of course, suggest that *all* people who are interested in this particular tax scheme are using it to combat Federal educational programs. In the Congressional setting, however, the correlation between the two is striking.

[15] At the time of this writing, the situation in Georgia and Alabama is in doubt, though in both States there has been court action.

[16] H. G. Good, *A History of American Education* (New York, 1956), pp. 536–537.

[17] We use the term "legend" because there are experienced and knowledgeable people who doubt its accuracy. They point to Senate floor discussion of the issue of discrimination in admissions and in particular to remarks by Senator Jacob Javits of New York. Senator Javits read into the record assurances from officials of the Department of Health, Education, and Welfare that the bill under discussion clearly established objective, fair basis for selection of beneficiaries, thus rendering unnecessary any language prohibiting the application of unjust grounds for selection. Both parties could be right. It would not be the first time that legislation was adopted with the support of diametrically opposed legislators, each confident the bill embodied his views.

[18] Frequently, advocates of this view make a distinction between those programs in which the law gives to the administering official a degree of latitude in choosing the benefiting participating institutions and those in which any given institution is "entitled" to benefits if it meets express provisions of the law. In the former instance they see

special grounds for withholding Federal funds from segregated institutions.

[19] Excerpt taken from speech presented by Mr. Metcalf, "Federal Aid for School Construction," February 6, 1956, *Congressional Record, House,* p. 2219.

[20] Interestingly, the Commission divided 3 to 3 on the question of withholding Federal funds from private institutions. Given the fact that citizens have access to the courts for the redress of wrongs in so far as public institutions are concerned, it seemed to many that the responsibility of the executive branch of the Federal Government was even greater in the private than in the public instance.

[21] The January, 1961, recommendations of the Civil Rights Commission called for ". . . executive or, if necessary, by Congressional action . . ." without indicating what factors might make Congressional involvement "necessary."

[22] This is not to say, of course, that there are not other ways of looking at the issue. The view that discriminatory practice in any of its many forms is incompatible with educational values is one.

CHAPTER FIVE

THE FUTURE DIMLY SEEN

When Thomas Jefferson recommended, in 1806, that education be placed "among the articles of public care," he could hardly have foreseen the extraordinary route by which, over a period of a century and a half, his recommendation would move toward adoption by the American people. Nonetheless, his words seem in retrospect to have been prophetic. The "circle" of education to which Jefferson felt the Federal Government should contribute was, he said, made up of parts, all of which "contribute to the improvement of the country, and some . . . to its preservation." To tailor the observation to the realities of mid-twentieth-century life, it would be necessary only to say that *all* the parts of the circle now contribute to the preservation of the country.

For the facts, some of which have been reported here, make amply clear that higher education, at least, is now acknowledged as a legitimate object of Federal concern. Much of that concern and its legitimacy stems directly from a growing conviction that the full circle of higher learning is intimately related to the preservation of the Nation. It is no longer appropriate to argue whether or not there is a Federal interest that should be expressed in the form of assistance. The questions that remain have to do with the extent and nature of the interest and the amount and kind of assistance. A group of distinguished educators and lay leaders put it this way, exactly 150 years after Thomas Jefferson's remarks: "In short, the

184

question at issue is not whether the federal government should have a role in higher education. That question was settled affirmatively in the nineteenth century and not seriously reopened. The question at issue is *what kind* of role the federal government should play in higher education." [1]

The answer to this question must rest on some notion of the Federal Government's interest in education. We have asserted the existence of such an interest, but have until now withheld any definition save that which emerges by inference from what the Government has in fact done. It is necessary, though, to try to capture that elusive concept of the "Federal interest," for from it will flow, it is to be hoped, a picture of what the Government will or should do in the future.

At the risk of seeming evasive, it could be said that the Federal interest in higher education is some part of a broader entity which, for want of a better term, might be called the "national interest." Viewed in one way, the traditional conception of the role of the Federal Government in any area of the society is that it is responsible for protecting, and promoting, that part of the national interest which other groups and individuals are unable, by themselves, to do. The scope of the Federal interest, in this sense, varies from subject to subject—it is coincident with the national interest in the field of military security; it has been virtually nonexistent in the promotion of the arts.[2] It varies, too, from time to time: the conception of the Federal interest in the stability of the economic system, as an example, underwent a drastic change in the 1930s.

The Federal interest in higher education is, we submit, changing as we watch it, and the change is in the direction of encompassing an ever-larger part of the broader national interest.

Stated broadly, the national interest in higher education is fairly clear. It consists in developing to the fullest the capacity of institutions of higher education to preserve, enlarge, and transmit the culture of man. Whatever enhances their ability to perform these functions promotes the national interest; whatever inhibits them weakens that interest. In loftier terms the national interest is that expressed at the dedication of The Johns Hopkins University: "Less misery among the poor, less ignorance in the schools, less bigotry in the temple, less suffering in the hospital, less fraud in business, less folly in politics."

In the postwar years the Federal interest has been focused intensively on a relatively small part of the total mission of—or by our definition, the national interest in—colleges and universities. The fact that the largest part of Federal activity has been motivated by a need for services and a concern for manpower rather than by the desire to support and bolster the educational system has no doubt produced that intensive focus.

The truly significant development of the last three or four years has been the sign of an enlargement of the Federal interest to coincide more nearly with the national interest. The sign, as some suggest, may be no larger than a man's hand on the horizon. But it is there, and it is visible in certain aspects of the National Defense Education Act and in the imminence of Federal assistance for the construction of academic facilities. We take these to be hopeful signs, for our view is that the Federal interest in higher education, properly conceived, coincides with the national interest.

Although the existence of a broadening Federal interest in higher education is manifest, the facts and factors treated in preceding chapters demonstrate that it would be exceedingly difficult to predict with any certainty the shape of future developments with regard to the expression of that interest. Nonetheless, there are certain discernible trends and tendencies that suggest general probabilities for the years immediately ahead.

Of course, politicians, pundits, and social scientists rediscover, periodically, the old truth that predicting the course of social affairs is a hazardous pastime. So numerous and so complex are the variables involved in almost any event that it is impossible even to know them all, much less to weigh or control them. Such considerations rarely daunt the intrepid though, for prediction is a principal instrument of control over one's environment. All intelligent people make plans of one kind or another, and what is planning if it is not a set of implied predictions that certain things will happen if certain other things can be made to happen first?

With all the appropriate qualifications, then, we believe that certain trends in Federal policy, evident now, are likely to continue, in some form, in the future, and that it is a responsibility of informed people to know what these are so that they may be shaped in desirable ways.

The Substance of Federal Policy

First, it seems clear that the historical emphasis on categorical problems will continue. The reasons for this are all around us and can be summarized in brief as follows: We have only begun to be aware of how complex our world is, physically and, even more, socially. The demands for the knowledge essential to survival in the world, not to mention progress, will multiply with each year, and institutions of higher education, as the bodies primarily charged with providing knowledge and with training those capable of using it and finding more, will feel these demands most heavily. The last twenty years have shown beyond any doubt that the National Government has been given the responsibility for mobilizing a major part of society's resources for this task in an increasing number of areas. For example, in the last ten to fifteen years, the Federal Government has come virtually to underwrite the research effort in the health sciences, in nuclear science and technology, in the space sciences, and in a host of other scientific areas. This will surely continue, for to say that categorical programs of support and purchase of services are here to stay is to say only that society needs what colleges and universities have to offer.[3]

Not only will such programs continue; there is every likelihood that their number will increase. In the past, furthermore, Federal programs of this kind have been largely scientific; in the future the social sciences are likely to be tapped in growing measure. Support is growing, for example, for a new Federal Department of Housing and Urban Affairs, as proposed by President Kennedy early in his administration. With the establishment of such a Department would come inevitably demands on the research potential of colleges and universities in the fields of sociology, economics, political science, city planning, and others. There is already evidence that there would be demands for student-assistance programs to train needed manpower in areas of interest to such a Department. A program of fellowships for students of city planning, to have been administered by the Housing and Home Finance Agency, was passed by the 86th Congress but vetoed by the President. The efforts of Senator Joseph Clark to pass similar legislation again, though frustrated in the 1961 Congressional session, are certain to persist.

The formation of a new department would add momentum to these developments, but whether one is actually established or not, the growing concern over the state of our cities is certain to be reflected in Federal policy and is equally certain to affect colleges and universities as a consequence.

If we could look forward to nothing more than these things, as important as they are, the picture would not be an entirely happy one. Running parallel, however, to the growing categorical programs, there is discernible a broadening trend in Federal activities, visible in several forms, that is most hopeful.

First, there is a tendency for programs that were originally narrowly conceived to become more general. The formation of the National Science Foundation, with its responsibilities for the development of basic science, generally, is an example. In recent years, the NSF has begun to exercise its long-latent authority in the area of the social sciences, as well. The Federal interest in the development of trained manpower, which started with an emphasis on special and highly technical skills, has developed into such broad student-assistance programs as the National Defense Student Loan Program and the fellowship program in the same Act, which embraces all basic fields of study. Indeed, as we have seen, the

Preamble to the National Defense Education Act states explicitly the national interest in the development of trained manpower, broadly construed.

Second, Federal programs will probably continue to broaden in their coverage of institutions. The dilemma of the administrators of special-purpose programs—whether to play to acknowledged strength or to build up new centers of strength—is most likely to be solved by doing both. The first legislative evidence of this was seen in the National Defense Graduate Fellowship Program, with its requirements for the development of additional facilities for graduate education and for wider geographic distribution of those facilities. At almost the same time, the National Science Foundation announced the inauguration of its Cooperative Fellowship Program, which guaranteed awards to a larger number of schools than participated in its existing programs. We have here a case in which political and educational considerations have combined to produce a broadening of Federal policy which could greatly extend the base of strength in higher education.

Third, Federal programs are likely to broaden in yet another way. If the preceding development can be called a horizontal extension of Federal activities, then there is likely, too, to be a vertical extension. Here we refer to a widening of the focus of attention from the graduate schools—the primary objects of research and manpower programs heretofore—to embrace undergraduate education as well. The form which this will take is still open to question. It is virtually certain, however, that the immensely popular loan program of the National Defense Education Act will be continued, and there is persistent interest in a national scholarship plan, although the educational reservations and political hurdles here continue to be formidable.[4]

Finally, it seems safe to say that we shall see shortly a program of assistance to colleges and universities in their capacity *as institutions* rather than as purveyors of needed services. Present indications are that this is most likely to take the form of a grant-in-aid and loan program for the construction of academic facilities. But growing concern for the institutions themselves may be reflected in a variety of ways other than new legislation. The simple easement of currently strict policies with regard to the payment of indirect, overhead costs on Federal contracts would be a most welcome evidence to the Nation's universities that the Government had moved from the role of tough bargainer to that of understanding patron. Further extension of an already evident trend toward bloc grants and longer-term underwriting of sponsored research will be additional evidence of the same. Within the recent past, the National Science Foundation has begun to make grants for unrestricted, institutionally determined research equal to 5 per cent of its grants for sponsored research. The National Institutes of Health launched its General Research Support Program in fiscal year 1962, under which grants ranging from $25,000 to $300,000 are made to universities for the "general strengthening" of medical and health research and training. All of this constitutes a growing respect for educational institutions as such.

These, then, seem to be the major trends in Federal policy and the ones that can be extrapolated into the future with the greatest confidence. Events do not move themselves, though, and it is by no means inevitable that the future will bring more enlightened policies—and we believe that the developments we have sketched would be enlightened. The process of making policy at the national level is a complicated and sensitive one, and the failure to use that process intelligently is the single most important obstacle to reasoned policies. We call it an obstacle because we believe that the process has not been intelligently used in the past. To do so in the future it will be necessary to change some perspectives and attitudes, something that is never easy to do. The changes, it should be said, must come on both sides—the Government and higher education.

The first changes must come in views as to the proper goals of Federal policies. In this connection it will be noted that we have not spoken of *a* Federal policy toward higher education. There is none, there never has been one, and none will ever exist, if we mean by the term a comprehensive scheme which embraces all Federal activities and into which new ones can readily be fitted.

What does exist is a set of programs and policies, from which, taken together, can be deduced a pattern. The search for the "master plan" is a vain one, and what is worse, in the course of it real and attainable goals are likely to be lost.

Two things at least are called for: From educators and others concerned with the future of higher education there should come a realistic set of priorities for action. These should be informed by the kind of toughness-with-vision that every good administrator uses in setting priorities for the allocation of his own institution's resources. It is time to drop the idea that the Government will make large grants of money to institutions to use in any way they see fit. Most schools cannot even get such money from private donors; it seems even less realistic to expect it from the Government.

What is needed from the Government is a point of view toward higher education that includes an end to the notion that institutions of higher education are self-regulating, self-feeding production machines that can be called on indiscriminately to produce goods and services without damage to the mechanism. To change from an urban to a rural metaphor, the Government cannot continue to skim the cream from the educational system unless it ensures, at the same time, the supply of milk. At present there is no mechanism within the Government to provide that point of view, and it is certain that one will not appear unprompted. We incline, therefore, to the idea of a body to act as the "educational conscience" of the Government, to provide informed comment and criticism on governmental activities and to feed ideas into the system. Some means, we believe, is necessary to introduce the notion of coherence into a system that, by nature and tradition, tends toward separation.

The Form of Organization

The Federal Government of the United States has grown to proportions and a degree of complexity that have sometimes invited ridicule. But the number of things that the Government does, and does well, justifies in the minds of most the need for a Federal bureaucracy. It seems reasonable to assume that as the Federal Government extends its areas of concern and adds to the swelling number of its functions, there will be further growth in the size and complexity of the Government structure. This is especially true of an area such as education, in which Federal activity is, as the record indicates, growing rapidly. This fact inevitably raises questions regarding the possibility of consolidation and the necessity of coordination among Federal programs in higher education.

In the light of developments sketched here, it would be unrealistic, to say the least, to expect any large-scale consolidation of educational activities within the Federal Government. Special-purpose programs, located in those agencies to which the purpose (or mission) rather than the device are of central importance, would lose much of their justification if they were removed from their parent agency. A program whose object is to strengthen the military defenses of the Nation should and certainly will remain within the defense establishment, even though it may impinge upon, or indeed affect profoundly, the Nation's colleges and universities. An effort to consolidate such programs into an educationally centered agency would do more than arouse the ire of the special-interest groups within higher education; it would inevitably diminish the effectiveness of the programs in reaching their essential objectives.

On the other hand, there are programs whose purposes are clearly related to educational needs and objectives, but which have been dispersed throughout the Government for essentially political reasons. There is some reason to believe that time may diminish the need for preserving these political distinctions and that a degree of consolidation among them may be hoped for. The College Housing Loan Program, for example, may not much longer require the political immunity that comes from its classification as a housing program, and it may be possible to acknowledge it for what it is, namely, a program of assistance to colleges and universities. Assuming that the political obstacles to this course of action can be overcome, there would be added benefit to the program by separating its fate from that of the highly controversial housing program.

Even if and when such acknowledgment is made, however, it will remain a question whether or not this program should be assigned to an educationally centered agency of the Federal Government. For one thing, the program has been well administered in both a housing and an education sense right where it is, and reasonable people can agree with Alexander Pope:

> Over forms of government let fools contest;
> What's best administered is best.

But an even more important factor in the decision to consolidate or not consolidate educationally directed programs is the attitude of educators themselves. At best, they are uncertain of the desirability of lodging programs of this sort in a single agency—presumably, the Office of Education in the Department of Health, Education, and Welfare—on at least two counts. In the first instance they have followed over the years a conscious policy of encouraging the dispersal of educational power within the Federal Government, the better to protect themselves against the dangers— real or imagined—of a strong central agency. This "Balkanization" has been justified in terms of the characteristic pluralism of American higher education:

> This is not to argue—as some have argued—that we need a highly integrated or coordinated federal program for higher education. Our higher education is by nature enormously complex, enormously diverse, serving many purposes and many functions. Any attempt to impose too much coordination upon federal

dealings with this system would ultimately reduce the diversity of the system itself. In our pluralistic society it is proper that the federal approach to higher education be pluralistic.[5]

Another reason for higher education's reluctance to encourage integration of Federal programs has, to be perfectly candid, stemmed from a lack of confidence in the U.S. Office of Education, the logical locus of such centralization. Leaders of the movement to create a National Science Foundation, with the responsibility for educational activities in the sciences, have recently acknowledged this motive openly, though it had been apparent to many for some time. That the creation of such a foundation might have been "the perfect formula for producing a legislated imbalance in higher education" seemed to them a lesser danger than entrusting the program to persons who did not have their professional confidence.

These, then, are some of the factors that caution against any expectation of streamlined administration of Federal programs affecting higher education. It appears that the mission-oriented approach of the Federal Government has coincided sufficiently with higher education's desire to deal with the Government on a fragmented basis to build into the present system a powerful degree of inertia.

On the other hand, there are indications that some shift in Federal arrangements can be anticipated. The broadening of individual Federal programs and the general broadening of the Federal concept of its interest in higher education would seem to ensure some changes. Assuming that some sort of basic program designed to strengthen higher education as such will be enacted during the next few years, then it is reasonable to assume as well that one major agency of the Government will emerge as a focal point of the Federal Government's interest in higher education. That agency presumably would be the U.S. Office of Education, whose experience with the National Defense Education Act seems to suggest that significant programs help to build quality staff, which in turn provides the professional confidence that is an apparent prerequisite to further responsibility.

As such an agency emerges within the Federal Government, certain other possibilities present themselves. It is not at all difficult to conceive of such an agency serving within the Federal structure as a spokesman for the Nation's long-term interest in higher education—a voice of conscience amid the babel of expedience. Given sufficient stature—and it is a fact of Government life that stature follows effective exercise of program responsibility, and not the reverse—such an agency could effectively monitor all Federal programs and their effects upon the Nation's system of higher education. It could advise other Federal agencies in such a way as to minimize the distorting, and even damaging, effects upon education of mission-oriented activities, and it could, in extreme cases, ring the alarm bell in reports to the President and/or the Congress. It could, in doing so, propose positive steps to modify or counteract the educational ill effects of carelessly drawn legislation and careless administration of programs. It cannot be emphasized too strongly that such a role within the Government, if it is to be played effectively, calls for stature within the Government and stature in the world of higher education. The former calls in turn for substantial experience and operating responsibility for Federal programs, and the latter calls for staff of high professional standing and broad perspective. Such an agency must therefore rank as a "pro" in the context both of the Government and of academic life. Nothing short of a conscious and concerted effort to create such an agency is likely to bring it into being.

Given such an agency, it would then be possible to think in terms of meaningful coordination of Federal programs in the field of higher education. A coordinating committee—an interagency committee such as the present Federal Council on Science and Technology—would stand a greater chance of succeeding in its efforts if it contained a strong voice speaking for the long-term Federal interest in education. Without this voice, such a committee is likely to do little more than consolidate a piecemeal Federal interest in parts of the Nation's system of higher education—to make the policy one of autonomous parts rather than of parts coordinated in the pursuit of a coherent point of view. Only a strong voice for the basic Federal (or national) interest in education can give to a coordinating effort the central purpose it needs and keep that purpose constantly before the participants.

There is a good deal of understandable skepticism, both in and out of Government, about coordinating committees. In the authors' view, the lack of success in most such efforts stems from the absence of a discernible focus or purpose to the coordinating effort and the want of a sufficiently strong voice to state the purpose convincingly and persistently. Had the National Science Foundation, for example, been given enough program responsibility to put it in the "big leagues" of Federal research and had it been given a solid place in the political structure of the Government (including access to the President's cabinet), we believe it could have carried out more effectively its charter to coordinate Federal scientific programs in the long-term national interest.

There are other ways of effecting coordination and of providing purpose to variegated programs. Among the most popular of these proposed alternatives is a national advisory group made up of persons outside the Government; another is a staff officer in the White House charged with the responsibility for coordination and, presumably, cloaked with the authority of the President to effect it. Each of these has certain attractive aspects. Chief among them is the greater visibility, in the form of public attention, that each would give to educational problems. We do not believe, however, that this virtue is sufficient to obscure the serious defects of the two proposals. It is our view that neither is a satisfactory substitute for a governmental agency, well staffed and long experienced. The task of looking after so vast an interest as that of the Federal Government in higher education is one that calls for extensive, full-time, professional attention. It is, as we have suggested, a lot to expect of a Federal agency; it is even more to expect of a parttime committee, however distinguished, or of a single top executive, however well qualified. Much of the coordination looked for among Federal programs does not require, either, the kind of imposition from above that would certainly color the recommendations or policies of a highly placed committee or executive; it will come best and most lastingly through the process of education itself—a more likely consequence of a soundly conceived interagency committee.

Perhaps it is unfair to talk of a national advisory committee or a Presidential advisor on education as an alternative to an effective governmental agency, concerned on a full-time basis with the problems of education. It is argued with some cogency that a committee or an advisor could be extremely helpful in creating a "climate of opinion" favorable to the consideration of serious educational problems and that this would strengthen rather than weaken the agencies of the Government whose full-time business is education.

As an ideal there is much to be said for this point of view, and it is certainly true that educational problems require greater public visibility and attention. If, however, these devices are viewed essentially as weapons in the competition for public attention, without influence over the substance of policy, one wonders about the quality of men who would be attracted to them. Conversely, to the extent that their power extends to policy, they must inevitably detract from the stature and authority of the regular agency which we believe is needed.

If visibility for educational problems is a matter of first priority, it can be provided best by the President himself through the powerful channels of communication at his command. Given the Presidential will to use the means at his disposal, there will be no lack of informed advisors within his official family—the Secretary of Health, Education, and Welfare, as an example—for him to call upon.[6]

The potentialities of a national advisory committee, on the other hand, suggest again the importance of the role to be played by *non*government groups and agencies in the formulation of Federal policy and the administration of Federal programs. Certainly, if the authors have made clear any conviction of theirs, it is that spokesmen for American higher education must make a greater effort to be heard. The "National Advisory Committee" and the "Council of Educational Advisors to the President" are beguilingly simple devices designed to bring this about. But apart from questions as to the extent to which the Office of the President can administer the affairs of the Government, or the extent to which interagency problems can be solved by a process of layering over with additional agencies, these proposals require careful scrutiny. Complex administrative and policy problems seldom yield to such appealingly simple solutions.

A body of nongovernment persons charged with the development of Federal policies affecting higher education would, of necessity, suffer from some of the shortcomings of previous, temporary bodies. It would presumably have to be representative [7] and would therefore be in danger of arriving at decisions that smack of the lowest common denominator; it would, perforce, devote part time to problems of full-time magnitude and complexity, and to do its job at all adequately it would have to rely on the work of a staff that approached in size and skill the kind of staff we have envisaged for a Federal educational agency.

But more basically, one must raise the question, "To what extent can 'nongovernment' conscientiously carry out the work of the Government?" Surely there is a need for top-level attention among educators to the policies and practices of the Federal Government; indeed, the "monitoring" mechanism suggested here should be duplicated within the ranks of higher education, if only on the theory that two consciences are more effective than one.[8] The question is whether or not these activities are to be carried on in the interests of higher education, with policies nurtured in the atmosphere of academic life, and then presented as recommendations to the Government, or whether they should be carried on for the Government and nurtured in the atmosphere of the Government where, as we have tried hard to suggest, some highly complicating forces—properly—come to bear.

There are strong arguments for the former, not the least of which is that it avoids any suggestion of collusion or surrender of integrity on the part of the Government or higher education. There are convincing instances in which highly regarded—even distinguished—educators have joined the Federal service, only to gain all too quickly the reputation of "company men"—the willing tools of the Government, forgetful of their loyalties to and interest in the academic community. They personify one dimension of the clouding effect of failure to distinguish between the total public interest and the public interest as it is served by one of society's mechanisms.

The danger that organized higher education could, by involving itself too closely in the structure of the Federal Government, open itself to a "company union" charge, has its counterpart for the Government itself. The American public quite properly looks to its Government for a degree of objectivity on matters of public policy that could *appear* to be compromised by too intimate association with identifiable elements of that society. Federal agencies are most severely criticized by thoughtful people when they seem to be representing the interests of their particular constituents rather than looking out for the public interest in matters under their jurisdiction. An acute case of this kind of schizophrenia has sometimes been found in the so-called independent regulatory commissions whose responsibility it is to regulate particular industries to protect the general interest of the public.

There is every reason to believe people will—if they do not already—look to a Federal agency for an impartial evaluation of the claims of the Nation's colleges and universities; some educators have themselves suggested that the most cogent argument for the elevation of education to cabinet status is to ensure its ability to act objectively in the face of competing claims and interests within the educational world. If evidence is needed that not all citizens regard educational organizations as being as objective as those agencies subject to constant public scrutiny, one need only look to Congressional investigations of alleged influence of philanthropic foundations in the formulation of public policy.

For a variety of reasons, therefore, it can be argued that the long-range development of Federal policy, so as to reflect the national *root interest* in higher education, can be brought about only through the conscious creation of a public agency whose specific charter is to speak for that interest—not to speak for higher education, but for the long-term Federal interest therein.

We do not mean to suggest here the polarization of Federal and educational interests. If, as we have expressed the hope, the Federal interest is to broaden into a national interest, it will be because the interests of Government are seen to coincide closely with the charter of education in a free society. It is not to minimize these common interests, but rather to encourage integrity in their identification, that the authors urge a more frank distinction between organized education and organized Government.

Federal, or national, policy in higher education cannot be developed soundly by any one of the parties to its development, separately. The "inside man"—the Government operator—however important his experience and perspective are, cannot (in our kind of society) be entrusted with the sole responsibility. The educator himself—the college president—on whom the responsibility for the actual conduct of higher education is most sharply focused, is inevitably a spokesman for an educational point of view; in the aggregate, college presidents are spokesmen for differences in point of view. The layman, upon whose ultimate judgment the total conduct of the Government rests, is relatively ill equipped to master the complex educational and governmental factors involved in the development of sound public policy.

Somehow, through some mechanism, these groups must jointly

participate in the identification of the Federal interest in higher education and in its expression. That extensive efforts have been made to effect such corporate judgment is evident in the scores of *ad hoc* and statutory advisory committees that now populate the structure of Federal agencies concerned with education. As one knowledgeable layman has observed, "We have tried just about every conceivable 'mix' of governmental and lay collaboration. Many of the things we have tried have been dismal failures, and many have been remarkably successful." From governing boards such as that of the National Science Foundation to panels of experts reviewing applications for research grants and graduate fellowships, the executive branch of Government abounds in experiments in three-dimensional policy development and execution.

Such experimentation is to be encouraged. The authors suggest that the most profitable avenues of experimentation are likely to be those that take into account certain realities of the situation. Prominent among these are the fact that Congress—for better or for worse—will exercise the final "lay" judgment on educational policy, in accordance with our conception of the Government. Another is that a pluralistic system of higher education such as ours is operated by persons and groups that must be regarded as competing parties-at-interest to the development of Federal policy. And a third is that a group of lay judges, faced with competing claims, should have access to a staff, if you will, of able people who are not themselves parties-at-interest, if it is to judge wisely and fairly.

It is considerations such as these that argue for the creation of a strong executive agency in the area of higher education. It must not be an agency remote from higher education, for it seeks to identify the broadest needs and requirements of higher education. Isolation, voluntary or enforced, from the interests of higher education would be disastrous. But independence of judgment and other evidences of integrity must characterize such an agency if it is to advise the public and its representatives objectively and fairly.[9] It is, to be sure, a delicate position or role to maintain as well as to describe, and it is reasonable to assume that a good deal of experimentation with—and change in—the "mix" will be necessary to its fulfillment. But in any combination of the ingredients their identity should not be lost.

Robert Frost has said it as well as anyone: "The separateness of the parts is at least as important as the connection of the parts."

The creation of a strong Federal agency would, of course, have implications for the posture of higher education itself. As already indicated, there would exist a need for continuous monitoring of Federal programs in the light of the interests of higher education itself. With the apparently inevitable extension of the pattern of special or categorical Federal programs, the ramifications of Federal activity will be complex beyond today's conception. Many of these implications will be "watchdogged"—not to say inspired— by the equally inevitable growth of counterpart organizations within higher education. This growth of specialized associations will increase the pressures for coordination among interests, much as it cries out for coordination within the Federal Government. The centripetal, fractionating effect of growing special interest will be felt all the way to the individual campus.

Just how successful the Nation's colleges and universities will be in finding means to speak as institutions and identify their broadest common interests is difficult to say. Achieving the much-sought-after ideal of union without unity or uniformity has proved exceedingly difficult to date, and it may be fair to say that it will be attained only as external pressures mount to a point where the surrender of uniqueness seems a lesser evil than surrender of independence. This may call only for separating the important characteristics of independence from the less important trappings or symbols of separateness.

What may, in the last analysis, constitute the basic adjustment of higher education to changing Federal actions—and the same may well be true for the Federal stance—will be modification of the spirit that permeates existing organizational patterns. A significant change in the attitude of higher education might or might not inspire structural or organizational change. It is after all the spirit and the substance that justify the form.

Perhaps the most basic change, therefore, and the one that must precede all the others, for it is a condition for the others, is a change in the attitude of educators toward the processes of the Government—toward the processes of politics, if you will. Governmental decisions, particularly legislative decisions, do not come automatically out of a universal recognition of the national welfare. Nor do they ordinarily happen by accident. Things happen in politics because people with interests to preserve and promote, and ideas to turn into programs, make them happen. Those who believe that the business of making things happen in politics is beneath their dignity or not worth their time are likely to be hurt.

The evidence to support this point is perfectly clear and directly relevant to higher education. One recent example is the oath and affidavit provisions of the National Defense Education Act. It was only several months after the Act was passed that most people in the academic community were even aware that the requirements existed—far too late, of course, to do anything but to sound injured and to agitate for repeal. It then turned out that essentially the same requirements were a part of other student-aid programs and had been for some time—eight years in the case of the National Science Foundation.[10] An observer not involved in the issue might well sympathize with the irritation of some Congressmen that the higher-education community—eight years after the fact—had suddenly discovered that it was being injured.

The evidence of recent years leads to the inescapable conclusion that the Congress will continue to legislate in areas affecting higher education and that executive agencies will continue programs already begun and have new ones added in the future. These things can be done well—that is, with an awareness of the interests of higher education—or they can be done poorly, without such an awareness. The only certainty is that they will be done. In large measure, the quality and wisdom of future actions depend on the willingness and the ability of people in higher education to communicate a reasoned and reasonable set of educational priorities to people in the Government. It depends further on the willingness and ability of people in higher education to pursue their interests *within the political arena* with consistency, energy, and intelligence.[11]

All of this assumes, of course, that education is in fact "among the articles of public care." It is the task of those who believe that it is to see to it that this care is discharged in ways that will do credit to all those who share it and will bring benefit to all who depend on it.

NOTES

[1] Annual Report of the Carnegie Foundation for the Advancement of Teaching, 1956–1957, p. 12.

[2] Even here the definition of the Federal interest has begun to change, as evidenced by the authorization of a national cultural center in Washington, D.C., and the growing interest in a national commission on the arts. A bill, sponsored by Representative Thompson of New Jersey, authorizing the establishment of such an advisory body, was reported out by the House Committee on Education and Labor in 1961, but defeated by a narrow margin in the closing days of the session.

[3] No doubt this has always been true, and in the broadest sense colleges and universities have always been shaped by what society has "wanted" from them. As one acute observer has said, "If our educational institutions had figured out a few centuries ago how to defend their 'integrity' against the unbalancing pressures of society, we would still be stuck with the *trivium* and *quadrivium*." A balance is struck, however, by each party exerting pressure against the other. The "integrity" of both is important, or else the result is a conquest rather than a balance.

[4] The plain fact of the matter is that opposition to Federal scholarships is aided and abetted by disagreement among supporters. Some

proponents have a humanitarian objective, others a manpower orientation, and still others seek to establish incentives for better academic performance. Such critical variables as financial need, state or institutional administration, categorical vs. general applicability, for example, are in disagreement among the supporters of Federal scholarships. The experience of the House Committee on Education and Labor in 1961 seemed to suggest that no substantial agreement could be reached on either the rationale or provisions of such a program.

Another idea, which has gained some popularity recently, is what might be called the "bounty proposal." In this scheme the Government would pay an institution a fixed amount of money for each student it graduated. In the format of a manpower concern, it would authorize unrestricted funds for general expenses of the Nation's undergraduate colleges. Lest this seem too improbable, it should be pointed out that the Defense Department in 1960 proposed just such a plan to apply to its ROTC graduates, and the Heald Commission in New York State offered the scheme, to cover all institutions in the State, as one of its major recommendations. We do not suggest that a "bounty plan" is likely to be enacted in the near future, nor do we endorse it; but we offer it as an indication that ingenious and responsible people are searching hard for more meaningful programs of educational assistance.

[5] Annual Report of the Carnegie Foundation for the Advancement of Teaching, 1956–1957, p. 24.

[6] The problem is in part a semantic one. A person serving on the staff of the White House and concerned with education could be an advisor to the President, going wherever and whenever necessary to develop his advice. As such, he could interfere seriously with the proper functioning of Government by, among other things, interposing himself between the President and those in Government charged both with advising the President and with carrying out his policies. On the other hand, he could serve in a more clearly staff capacity actually to facilitate the President's access to his advisors, and vice versa. To the extent that such a staff person contributed to the fullest exercise of Presidential concern for and interest in Federal educational programs, we should hardly question the desirability of his appointment; to the extent that he stood in place of the President or between the President and his existing educational appointees, we should regard his appointment as regrettable.

[7] To the extent that such a body were constituted of anything other than representative educators, it would suffer, too, from the skepticism of some educators, as the following observation suggests (from a background memorandum prepared for the December 10, 1960, "Seminar on Federal Relationships"): "Some interested groups are projecting the image of a new super-commission, made up of educators and friends of education with such great stature that when they speak they can sway the public mind and the Congress. These men would presumably speak with a strong and single voice on issues concerning which individual educators, educational institutions, and educational organizations may be divided. It is the hope that even though they represent nobody they will able to persuade everybody."

[8] It may be desirable, if unnecessary, to state the obvious here. A Federal educational agency, however competent and objective, is an arm of the executive branch and answerable, therefore, to the President and subject to his policy direction. The existence of an alert nongovernment organization has obvious value in this context in ensuring that the truth is not seared in the heat of politics or compressed by the limitations of an individual executive.

[9] A similar recommendation was embodied in the 1961 report of the U.S. Office of Education's Committee on Mission and Organization, "A Federal Education Agency for the Future." Largely obscured by public clamor over what was termed by some a "blueprint for a Federal takeover of education," this particular recommendation had a mixed reception. Public school critics betrayed some anxiety, but higher-education leaders gave no indication that they considered themselves endangered by a strong Federal agency.

[10] Some educators have made much of the fact that the concept of institutional administration written into some features of the NDEA required the institutions to extract the oath in behalf of the Government, and thus did violence to institutional integrity. Assuming that the point has some validity, it hardly seems sufficiently important to justify the rejection of one program and the tolerance of another when both embody a requirement so fundamentally at odds with academic values.

[11] A recent and otherwise thoroughly admirable report (*Report of the Committee on the University and World Affairs,* December 1960, p. 51) by a distinguished group of educators and lay leaders contains the following sentence: "The universities' understandable reluctance

to make the case for international education in the halls of Congress has too often been interpreted by Congressmen as an indication that existing arrangements for the use of universities and existing levels of university support were adequate to the national need."

The authors agree with the substance of the statement but do not find the universities' "reluctance" at all "understandable."

INDEX

209